THE
EUROPEAN
DEBT
CRISIS

pac ps

Pacific Publishing Studio

CONTENTS

Introduction

Seventeen of the European Union's 27 member states share an economic and monetary union (EMU) with the euro as a single currency. Based on a gross domestic product (GDP) and global trade and investment shares comparable to those of the United States, these countries (collectively referred to as the Eurozone) are a major player in the world economy and can affect U.S. economic and political interests in significant ways. Given its economic and political heft, the evolution and future direction of the Eurozone is of major interest to Congress.

Uncertainty about the future of the Eurozone began in early 2010 as a result of the onset of a sovereign debt crisis in Greece. Subsequently, concerns spread that Ireland, Portugal, Spain, and Italy also lacked sustainable fiscal positions. Fearing possible defaults, markets began demanding substantially higher interest rates for their bonds. The debt problems of these countries, while varying from case to case, now constitute a serious risk to the European banking system, the viability of the euro, and the European integration process. Anemic growth in the Eurozone with a mild recession forecast for 2012 is compounding the debt and banking problems. Standard & Poor's downgrade of the credit ratings of France, Italy, and seven other European countries on January 13, 2012, served as an additional reminder that the crisis is far from over.

One important cause of the crisis stems from flaws in the architecture of the currency union, including the fact that the EMU provides for a common central bank (the European Central Bank or ECB), and thus a common monetary policy, but leaves fiscal policy up to the member countries. Weak enforcement of fiscal discipline, over time, facilitated rising public debts in some of the countries. Locked into the euro, individual members cannot inflate their way out of large public debt or devalue their currency to make their exports more competitive.

In response, European leaders and institutions have combined measures to ease the debt crisis with financial assistance packages for Greece, Ireland, and Portugal. The most highly indebted Eurozone members have been forced to cut government spending and programs and to raise taxes to improve their fiscal positions. A financial assistance facility, the European Financial Stability Facility, has been created to help stabilize the crisis. The ECB has made large purchases of these countries' public debt in order to calm markets, and in December 2011 provided a huge infusion of credit into the banking system. But many observers are now calling for more fundamental solutions, such as the issuance of Eurobonds, along with other institutional reforms that could provide a stronger fiscal foundation to the monetary union.

The reforms, if implemented, could strengthen the foundation of the Eurozone and bolster confidence in the euro. At the same time, a number of factors could weaken or perhaps even undermine the sustainability of the Eurozone. Public support in fiscally sound Eurozone countries, such as Germany, Finland, and the Netherlands, for resource transfers to highly indebted countries is weak. If the Eurozone survives largely in its current form or strengthens, the impact on U.S. interests is likely to be minimal. However, if Greece or any other Eurozone member were to default on its debt, it could lead to another wave of credit freeze-ups and instability in the European banking sector that weakens a slow growing U.S. economy. Longer term, if the Eurozone were to break up in a way that undermines the functioning of Europe's single market, or resurrects national divisions, the impact on U.S. economic and political interests could be deeper and more damaging.

The Future of the Eurozone and U.S. Interests

By
Raymond J. Ahearn, Coordinator
Specialist in International Trade and Finance

James K. Jackson
Specialist in International Trade and Finance

Derek E. Mix
Analyst in European Affairs

Rebecca M. Nelson
Analyst in International Trade and Finance

What has become known as the Eurozone crisis began in early 2010 when financial markets were shaken by heightened concerns that the fiscal positions of a number of Eurozone countries, beginning with Greece, were unsustainable. Fears that a possible Greek default could spread to other Eurozone countries, particularly Ireland, Italy, Portugal and Spain, were exacerbated by revelations of banking sector weaknesses and a delayed policy response from European leaders and institutions. After extended negotiations, European leaders and the International Monetary Fund (IMF) agreed in May 2010 to provide funding for a €110 billion (about $158 billion) loan facility for Greece and a broader stabilization fund for other euro area countries should they require loans.1 Both loan packages were backstopped by various forms of assistance from the U.S. Federal Reserve Board (FRB) and the IMF.2 The Greek bail-out was followed in December 2010 by a €67.5 billion (about $97 billion) rescue package for Ireland, and a €78 billion (about $112 billion) loan for Portugal in May 2011. In July 2011, a second financial assistance package totaling €109 billion (about $157 billion) was agreed to for Greece.3 In the most recent EU summit on December 8-9, 2011, EU leaders announced a number of new policy measures, including a fiscal compact and extension of bilateral lines of credit from European countries to the IMF, to address the Eurozone crisis.4

These policy responses, resulting from nearly 15 "crisis summits" over the past two years have contained but not resolved the crisis. Standard & Poor's downgrade of the credit ratings of France, Italy, and seven other Eurozone members on January 13, 2012, was based, in part, on the view that European leaders are moving too slowly to strengthen the monetary union as the region heads into its second recession in three years.5 The same day suspension of negotiations between Greece and its creditors (commercial banks and other private holders of Greek debt) on accepting large losses to make its debt more manageable only added to the concern that the crisis is far from over.6

Some analysts believe that European leaders need to provide more financial resources to defend countries such as Italy and Spain against contagion, provide more liquidity to under-capitalized European banks, enact stricter rules to prevent governments from overspending, and provide more debt relief to the insolvent Greek government. Other observers emphasize that the Eurozone is institutionally flawed and that efforts to fix this flaw with more rigid rules will not work. This argument is that a monetary union without a fiscal union is unstable and that only common fiscal institutions, such as joint debt issuance and a pooling of budgetary resources, can ensure the Eurozone's survival.

European policymakers have, in fact, focused on the need to address flaws in the architecture of the Economic and Monetary Union (EMU) of the European Union (EU).7 Most observers believe that reform of the currency union is needed in order to bolster the euro and avoid another fiscal crisis triggered by public debt and government deficits. How the members of the Eurozone address this overriding challenge to bolster the viability and stability of the currency union has added significance. Unlike in countries such as Argentina or Mexico, where currency crises did not bring into question the existence or survival of the state, the euro bears weight in terms of Europe's political aspirations for an "ever closer union." As viewed by German Chancellor Angela Merkel, "the currency union is ... a question, no more or less, of the preservation of the European idea ... for if the euro fails, Europe fails."8

A broad range of views exists on the future of the Eurozone. Some academics and journalists maintain that fears about the long-term viability of the Eurozone are exaggerated. The most optimistic, in fact, see the crisis as an opportunity to advance the idea of an "ever closer union" by pursuing greater economic integration and joint coordination of fiscal policy on the European level. Other observers maintain that a potential break-up of the currency union, in part or in whole, cannot be ruled out, particularly given the difficulties a number of member governments are having in servicing their debt. While such a development would not necessarily lead to the demise of the European Union, most observers agree that a break-up would be destabilizing. A middle-ground perspective holds that Europe has the option to muddle through the crisis by introducing a combination of liquidity facilities and reforms that will lower fiscal deficits and raise economic growth in financially troubled member states.9

The Obama Administration, Federal Reserve (Fed), and Congress have been actively engaged in monitoring and working towards an orderly resolution of the Eurozone crisis. President Obama and Treasury Secretary Timothy Geithner reportedly have been in close contact with European leaders, urging them to take decisive action to resolve the crisis.

The Federal Reserve on September 15, 2011 reactivated dollar loans or liquidity swap lines with the ECB in an effort to ensure that European banks do not incur any temporary shortages of liquidity.10 The 112th Congress has held five hearings to date on various aspects of the crisis and its implications for the United States.11

5

A major U.S. concern is that a sovereign default by Greece or another member of the Eurozone or the collapse of a major European financial institution, could ignite a wave of credit freeze-ups that would spillover to U.S. and global financial markets and serve as a major shock to the U.S. stock market and economy. An additional U.S. concern is that the slowing Eurozone economy, along with a depreciating euro, will adversely affect U.S exports and earnings of U.S. companies.12

Background on the Economic and Monetary Union (EMU)

EMU officially stands for Economic and Monetary Union, but it also commonly referred to as the European Monetary Union. EMU is the agreement among participating countries of the European Union to adopt a single currency, the euro, and a common monetary policy set by a common central bank, the ECB.

Origins, Rationale, and Economic Significance

The origins of EMU are closely linked with the international monetary system established after World War II.13 As part of the post-war reconstruction efforts, countries returned to a gold standard and created a fixed, but adjustable, system of international exchange rates based on a fixed exchange rate between the U.S. dollar and the price of gold. The goal was to provide international monetary stability, facilitate trade, and prevent the competitive devaluations, unstable exchange rates, and protectionist trade policies of the interwar years. While European leaders had begun the process of economic integration immediately following World War II, consideration of monetary union did not begin in earnest until the international monetary anchor provided by the dollar-gold standard collapsed in 1971 and a new wave of currency instability emerged amidst divergent national policy responses to several 1970s economic shocks, including the oil crisis.

In 1979, the nine member countries of the European Economic Community (EEC) created the European Monetary System (EMS). The EMS introduced fixed but adjustable exchange rates among participating countries' currencies in order to keep fluctuations of their exchange rates within acceptable bands. In 1988, the European Commission, then led by Jacques Delors, chaired a committee which proposed a three-stage plan to reach full economic union. The plan included the establishment of a European central bank and a single currency that would replace national currencies.

The EMU officially began on January 1, 1999, when 11 EU members pegged their currencies at a fixed exchange rate in preparation for adoption of a common currency, the euro. Participating countries have a common central bank, the European Central Bank (ECB), and by extension a common monetary policy. Fiscal policy, or decisions about spending and taxation were left to the individual member states, subject to the 1997 Stability and Growth Pact.

The primary rationale for the EMU was to provide momentum for political union, a long-standing goal of many European policymakers. Germany and France, Europe's largest economies, played the lead role in establishing the EMU, but they have not always agreed on the management and direction of the single currency. Most observers believe that Germany's initial support for monetary union was motivated more by political than economic interests—former Chancellor Helmut Kohl saw the currency union as an important way to anchor Germany securely in a united Europe. French leaders, on the other hand, are thought to have viewed the currency union as a key step to increasing French influence within Europe. Each country subsequently had different priorities in guiding the development of the monetary union. Germany has insisted that the Eurozone be anchored in a culture of tight money, low inflation policy, and fiscal discipline. Accordingly, the ECB's overriding commitment to price stability is thought to reflect German preferences. For its part, France has pushed for more flexibility in European monetary policy and for more political control over the inflation-fighting ECB.[14]

Although political goals were the driving force in the move towards monetary union, discussions of EMU also focused heavily on its economic costs and benefits. Generally, European monetary union was expected to make Europe's economy more efficient, thereby raising the living standards of Europe. For example, it would eliminate the transaction costs of changing one currency

7

into another, which would benefit both consumers and producers. Additional economic benefits included lowering the cost of trading goods by removing exchange rate risk and currency conversion fees and by facilitating price comparisons of goods and services across national borders. Cost savings that arise from greater competition also induce direct investment from non-Eurozone countries as foreign firms attempt to locate facilities within the Eurozone area to access a larger market. Proponents of the EMU also wanted the euro to become one of the reserve currencies of international finance, alongside the dollar and the yen.15

The now 17 members of the Eurozone have considerable economic heft. Comprising some 320 million people, the gross domestic product (GDP) of the entire Eurozone area was $12.2 trillion in 2010,16 or about 19% of world GDP. By comparison, the GDP of the United States in 2010 was slightly larger at $14.6 trillion. Within the Eurozone, economic weight is heavily concentrated in a few large countries. More than 76% of the Eurozone's total GDP is accounted for by just four countries (Germany, France, Italy, and Spain). In contrast, the Eurozone's five smallest countries (in decreasing size: Slovakia, Slovenia, Luxembourg, Cyprus, and Malta) accounted for less than 2% of the Eurozone's overall GDP in the same year.

The Eurozone is also a major player in the world economy. As a whole, it accounted for 29% of total world exports; 28% of world imports; and 23% of world net inflows of foreign direct investment (FDI) in 2010.17 The United States also has a strong bilateral economic relationship with the Eurozone.18 With respect to merchandise trade, U.S. exports to Eurozone members totaled $176.7 billion in 2010, representing 14% of total U.S. exports of goods. Likewise, the value of U.S. imports of goods from the Eurozone in 2010 was $242.7 billion, or 13% of total U.S. imports.19 In terms of capital flows, U.S. investors on net repatriated $180.6 billion dollars from the Eurozone in 2010.20

Key Provisions of the EMU

The blueprint for the EMU was formalized in provisions of the 1992 Maastricht Treaty, the founding document of the present-day European Union. The Treaty established the conditions, or "convergence criteria," that countries are required to meet before they join the EMU.21 By requiring the members to adhere to similar economic policies, the convergence criteria are meant to promote more balanced economic growth and development among the various members of the Eurozone. This, in turn, was thought to make it easier for diverse economies to share a single currency.

EU Treaties

The Treaty on European Union (TEU or the Maastricht Treaty) is the founding document of the modern European Union. Together, the TEU and the 1957 Treaty establishing the European Economic Community (also known as the Rome Treaty or the EEC Treaty, and recently re-named the Treaty on the Functioning of the European Union, or TFEU) define the objectives and principles of the EU and set out the EU's institutional architecture and organizational rules. The Lisbon Treaty, which entered into force in December 2009, is the most recent treaty amending these documents.

As an integral part of the EMU, a European Central Bank (ECB) was established to set monetary policy independent of any political influence. The ECB together with the central banks of all the members of the European Union form the European System of Central Banks, or ESCB, which is charged by statute with maintaining price stability as its primary objective. The formulation of price stability as a primary ESCB objective, compared to the U.S. Federal Reserve's multiple mandates of price stability, full employment, and moderate long-term interest rates, was a German pre-condition for sacrificing the Deutsche mark.22

There was no provision in the Maastricht Treaty to allow the ECB to act as a lender of last resort to Eurozone members in the case of a financial crisis. According to the EMU's design, each member must finance its deficits by itself. A "no-bail-out" clause explicitly stipulates that neither the European Union nor any member state is liable for or can assume the debts of any other member state.23 However, EU financial assistance is allowed in case of "severe difficulties caused by natural disasters or exceptional occurrences beyond the control of a member state."24

9

For the mutual assurance and stability of the currency, all members are constrained in their ability to adopt independent fiscal policies by the Protocol on Excessive Deficit Procedure (EDP) and the Stability and Growth Pact (SGP). The EDP is a procedure under which member states are obliged to avoid excessive deficits in national budgets.25 The SGP, agreed to in 1997, was intended to deepen multilateral surveillance and "speed up and clarify" implementation of the EDP.26

Soon after the SGP took effect in 1999, EU members began criticizing the rules-based approach of the Pact for being too stringent and they questioned whether the rules could be enforced. In 2003, the weaknesses of the Pact were exposed when the European Council voted against applying the punitive procedures under the EDP to France and Germany, which had experienced rising levels of government debt. Some EU members argued that the Pact focused too heavily on the rules-based percentage guidelines without regard for the circumstances under which a government's level of debt or its deficit spending may rise, for instance as a result of a temporary increase in government spending to counter an economic downturn.27

In 2005, the EU members adopted a number of changes to the SGP. These changes made enforcement more flexible to take into account the economic conditions of the member states, and other factors. For example, the modified Pact provides for each EU member to develop its own medium-term objectives to bring its deficit spending and its debt level into compliance based on the unique economic conditions of each member. The changes also allow EU members to avoid the corrective measures in cases where their annual fiscal deficit exceeds 3% of GDP, if they can demonstrate that the deficit is caused by "exceptional and temporary" circumstances.

Design Challenges

From the start of the euro area, various academics and policymakers argued that a single currency for many different economies would face numerous challenges and some even argued that it was bound to fail. According to these critics, a big weakness of the project was the lack of a common fiscal policy to support it. This, in turn reflected the fact that it was a currency with a central bank but without a government that has taxation and spending authority. The creation of the euro also meant that members of the Eurozone lost their ability to use monetary and exchange rate policy tools as a way to respond to changes in economic conditions.28

The loss of monetary and exchange rate tools, combined with a lack of a common fiscal policy, creates vulnerabilities and tensions because members of the Eurozone are constrained in how they respond to economic shocks such as a recession. Countries are different and in a recession are likely to experience different unemployment rates. In a currency union, the central bank will set a common interest rate that may end up too high for the high unemployment country (resulting in lost employment and output), and too low for the low unemployment country (resulting in excess spending and consumption), exacerbating the business cycle in both countries.

Despite these costs, joining a currency union may be advantageous as long as there are adjustment mechanisms that ensure that the benefits of membership such as lower transaction costs and exchange rate certainty exceed the costs. These adjustment mechanisms, in the absence of a common federal budget and robust transfer mechanisms from countries experiencing booms to the countries experiencing recessions, include labor and capital mobility and wage and price flexibility. For example, the unemployment disparities could be reduced if workers from a country with high unemployment relocated to the one with low unemployment. Or, relative labor costs could fall in the high unemployment country to attract investment and create new jobs. In the absence of viable adjustment mechanisms, there are likely to be strains and tensions within a currency union.29

The functioning of the dollar in the U.S. economy, despite major differences among its 50 states, is facilitated by adjustment mechanisms that are either absent or deficient in the Eurozone. For example, U.S. unemployed workers move much more freely from Maine to Minnesota than do European unemployed workers from Spain to Slovenia because of factors such as language or common regulations. Prices of basic consumer durables vary little among the U.S. states but can be substantial among the members of the Eurozone. And the federal government in Washington

11

collects roughly two-thirds of all taxes and provides net fiscal transfers to states with temporarily falling incomes. No such substantial fiscal transfers occur in the Eurozone.30

Just as critical as the lack of a common federal budget to transfer resources from countries experiencing booms to countries experiencing recessions, the single currency can weaken the market signals that would otherwise warn a member that its fiscal deficits were becoming excessive. When a country with an excessive deficit needs to raise taxes and cut government spending, as is the case in many Eurozone countries now, the resulting contraction in output and employment cannot be moderated by a devaluation that increases exports and decreases imports. These shortcomings or design flaws inherent in the architecture of the currency union played a role in the sovereign debt crisis that hit Greece and several other Eurozone members in early 2010 and are discussed in the next section.

Economic Imbalances and Adjustment Mechanisms within the Eurozone

At the time of the euro's launch in 1999, a number of economists predicted that the monetary union would not survive because of shortcomings in its architecture. This section describes (1) the persistent economic imbalances that are at the heart of the current crisis; and (2) how the imbalances are related to the institutional constraints of the monetary union itself, particularly the lack of adequate adjustment mechanisms that can bridge the gap in competitiveness between the Eurozone's wealthy northern countries and the more spendthrift periphery.

Imbalances within the Eurozone

When the euro was introduced, many economists expected that the national economies within the Eurozone would achieve additional convergence. However, many of the Eurozone economies have remained quite different or have actually diverged in a number of dimensions since the euro was introduced over a decade ago. This divergence is generally thought to have occurred between two groups of countries within the Eurozone: the Northern European countries, including Austria,

Belgium, Germany, Finland, France, Luxembourg, and the Netherlands; and a group of mostly Southern European countries, including Greece, Ireland, Italy, Portugal, and Spain. These latter five countries are often referred to by the acronym "GIIPS."

Much of the money that the GIIPS borrowed to finance trade and budget deficits came from banks located in the Eurozone, particularly French and German banks. The exposure of French and German banks to the GIIPS rose from $357.2 billion in December 1999 to $1.6 trillion in December 2009, an increase of more than 450%.31 In sum, the net borrowers (the GIIPS) were being financed by the net savers (Northern European countries).

Adjustment Mechanisms

Differences between the economies of Northern Europe and the GIIPS can be attributed to a number of factors, including policy choices.32 For example, Germany's export-led economic strategy and commitment to wage moderation is often cited as a factor for its low costs of production and trade surpluses.

However, many have suggested that the imbalances are caused by the institutional arrangements of the currency union itself and its inadequate adjustment mechanisms. This argument typically proceeds as follows:33 After the GIIPS adopted the euro, investors viewed these countries as safer destinations for investment, and the interest rates paid by the GIIPS on their government bonds fell to the interest rates paid by Northern European countries. As a result, interest rates in the GIIPS were far too low, leading to distorted investment decisions and ultimately overinvestment in a number of sectors. As private sector borrowing and demand increased, the GIIPS launched investment projects to allow growth to take place with less inflation. This, in turn, required increased borrowing, particularly from banks in Northern European countries, and contributed to larger government budget deficits.

Capital inflows into the GIIPS fueled domestic demand, leading to high levels of growth, but also to inflation. Increasing prices in the GIIPS reduced their competitiveness, and consequently, caused the GIIPS to start running current account deficits. 34 Each year's current account deficits added to the public and private aggregate debt of the GIIPS. As part of this process, the GIIPS accumulated foreign debt which rose close to 80% of GDP.35

Meanwhile, most Northern European economies did not face dramatic reductions in their interest rates upon joining the Eurozone and did not have substantial increases in capital inflows. Combined with fiscal policies that aimed to contain domestic demand, the Northern European countries as a result had lower inflation and remained more competitive than their GIIPS counterparts. Partly due to their relative competitiveness, the Northern European countries were able to export to the GIIPS and run large current account trade surpluses.36

Some suggest that being in the Eurozone constrained the ability of the GIIPS governments to respond to growing divergences from the Northern European countries.37 For example, if the GIIPS countries had not been in the Eurozone, they could have reduced their trade deficits through currency depreciation. Likewise, the GIIPS countries could have raised interest rates to slow economic growth in response to a potentially over-heating economy. But as members of the Eurozone, neither devaluation nor an increase in interest rates is an option.

The GIIPS countries did retain some control over their fiscal policy and could have reined in government spending or raised taxes in order to curb consumption. Such a policy could have freed up resources for payments to foreign creditors.

However, the low interest rates resulting from Eurozone membership increased the attractiveness of government deficit spending, and the GIIPS countries generally borrowed, running budget deficits. Alternatively, given that inflation was twice as high in the GIIPS countries than the EMU average, real interest rates (i.e., nominal rates minus inflation) were extremely low, thereby discouraging savings and causing private firms and households to run up debt to finance consumption and housing construction, especially in Spain and Ireland.38

Given their membership in the Eurozone, the GIIPS are left with using deflation (decreases in wages, incomes, and prices) in order to reduce their trade deficits. However, deflation may have little beneficial effect on the foreign debt positions of most of the GIIPS if they all pursue the same strategy simultaneously. This is because the negative effects on economic growth and employment could be compounded, weakening the economies of the GIIPS to the point where their debt-to-GDP ratios continue to rise.39

In sum, the trade imbalances between the Northern countries and GIIPS provide evidence that the EMU's internal adjustment mechanisms are not working well. Whatever labor mobility and price flexibility that exists in the Eurozone, combined with limited fiscal transfers, did not prevent the accumulation of persistent trade imbalances and the current economic crisis. While improved labor mobility and price flexibility may be long-term solutions, European leaders and institutions are now considering a range of proposals to increase fiscal coordination and integration as the best way to shore-up the EMU's institutional shortcomings.

Eurozone Crisis Measures and Reform Proposals

Beginning in May 2010, European leaders and institutions adopted an unprecedented package of emergency measures to halt rising financial market tensions stemming from concern about the fiscal solvency of Greece and several other Eurozone countries. This section briefly discusses the crisis measures adopted to defuse the crisis and the reform proposals for economic governance and economic policies.

Financial Assistance to Greece, Portugal, and Ireland

Current concerns about the sustainability of domestic finances in several Eurozone countries began in early 2010 when investor sentiment turned against Greece, which had borrowed heavily in international capital markets over the past decade. Analysts argue that this borrowing was necessary to support high government spending, weak revenue collection, structural rigidities, and declining competitiveness.40 Access to capital at low interest rates after adopting the euro and weak enforcement of EU rules concerning debt and deficit ceilings helped set the stage for the current sovereign debt crisis.41

To date, Greece, Ireland, and Portugal have received significant financial assistance packages from the IMF and Euro area and EU fiscal facilities. The ECB has also contributed extensively to

European economic stability, actively intervening to support European governments and banks. Despite this support, concerns increased that the crisis could spread to the larger European economies, including Italy and Spain. Investor concerns about the likelihood of default in Greece and the other countries receiving financial assistance, as well as doubts about the ability of European authorities to agree on sufficient economic reforms, pushed the cost of issuing European sovereign debt up sharply for most Eurozone members except Germany.42

New EU Financing Facilities

The primary institutions available for providing emergency financial support to European governments and financial institutions, in addition to national authorities, are the European Financial Stabilization Mechanism (EFSM), the European Financial Stability Facility (EFSF), and the ECB. The IMF is also expected to make contributions as well as play a coordinating role, as it has much expertise in financial surveillance and putting together sovereign debt packages.43

European Financial Stability Mechanism
The EFSM is a €60 billion supranational EU balance of payments loan facility created in 2010 and available to any EU member country facing financial difficulties. It is similar in design to an existing €50 billion EU balance of payments facility that can only be drawn on by non-Eurozone EU member nations.44 Since 2008, Hungary, Latvia, and Romania have borrowed from this facility as part of joint EU-IMF economic adjustment programs.

Under the EFSM, the European Commission is allowed to raise up to an additional €60 billion on the international capital market by issuing bonds individually and collectively backed by all 27 EU member states.45 EFSM loans require a qualified majority vote of the Council of the EU. The borrowing nation would be subject to economic conditionality supervised by the European Commission, which would decide at regular intervals whether sufficient economic progress has been made to warrant the continued release of funds. Funds are available immediately and there is no sunset date for the EFSM. Beginning in January 2011, several bond offerings have been placed to partially fund the Ireland and Portugal assistance packages.

European Financial Stability Facility

European leaders decided to provide the majority of the initial rescue package, up to €440 billion (about $573 billion), in a temporary three-year crisis prevention facility, the so-called European Financial Stability Facility (EFSF), outside of the EU system. The EFSF has been established under Luxembourg law as a limited liability corporation.46 This allows participating countries to have greater discretion over the use of the facility's resources—decisions are made by a board of directors from participating countries instead of the European Commission—and to limit their liability to the amount of their individual guarantee. The amount of a country's guarantee is to be derived from their respective contributions to the paid-in capital of the ECB.

The EFSF depends on the credit rating of it guarantors to raise funds in capital markets, which it then lends to weaker members of the Eurozone at a small mark-up. On January 16, 2012, Standard & Poor's lowered the fund's credit rating from triple A to AA+ following earlier downgrades of France and Austria. As these two countries account for some 40% of the credit guarantees underlining the EFSF, this action could force the facility to pay higher premiums for its capital. To date the EFSF has contributed €43.7 billion to Ireland and Portugal and is expected to contribute another €150 billion to help underwrite a second Greek bail-out.47 The EFSF was expected to be replaced by a permanent lending facility, the European Stability Mechanism (ESM), after it expires in 2013. At the December 2011 Summit, leaders announced that this timeline would be accelerated to July 2012 so that it could overlap with the EFSF for a year. The S&P downgrade of the EFSF could reinforce this effort. The ESM will be comprised of €80 billion in paid-in capital contributions from Eurozone members, as opposed to the guarantees underlying the EFSF. In theory, this should make the ESM more robust, but this fund still must clear several legislative hurdles if it is to be up and running by mid-2012. And even then some analysts believe that for the ESM to be credible in the event larger European countries like Italy or Spain need to borrow from it, the fund would have to be increased five-fold, from its current €500 billion ceiling to at least €2.5 trillion.48

European Central Bank Response

Along with the creation of the EFSM and the EFSF, the European Central Bank has implemented several crisis-response measures to improve European financial stability. Arguably the most important of these measures is the ECB's decision to purchase European sovereign debt outright in the secondary markets. This was a significant policy reversal for the ECB, which had long viewed interventions in sovereign debt markets as compromising its independence, and a diversion from its core mandate of price stability. However, as it required several months to legally establish the EFSM and the EFSF, the ECB was able to provide immediate support following the worsening of the crisis in early May. The ECB began interventions on May 10, 2010, purchasing €16.5 billion of Eurozone sovereign debt.49 It is believed that the ECB is now among the largest holders of Greek, Italian, and Portuguese debt. Given a sharp increase in buying beginning in August 2011, the ECB as of mid-year 2011 held €143 billion of European sovereign debt.50

In December 2011 the ECB provided unusually flexible liquidity support to Eurozone banks. In what has been called the biggest infusion of credit ever into the banking system, the ECB awarded 523 banks with €489 billion euros (about $639 billion) in loans at the average benchmark interest rate – currently 1 percent—over a three year period. The ECB hopes that the banks will use the money to help them keep lending to companies and households, and possibly purchase sovereign debt that is being sold this year. In theory, the banks by borrowing at one percent could use the money to lend at much higher rates to European governments. But given ongoing fears of possible defaults, it is unclear whether the banks will consider increasing their exposure to government bonds as being too risky,51

Other ECB policy measures include the reactivation of temporary liquidity swap lines with the U.S. Federal Reserve. In addition to the ECB, the Fed re-activated temporary reciprocal currency agreements, known as swap lines, with the Bank of Canada, the Bank of England, Bank of Japan, and the Swiss National Bank.52 The swap lines with the Federal Reserve provide foreign central banks with a source of dollar financing should such immediate liquidity be needed.

Economic Governance Reforms

Crisis response measures have succeeded in calming financial markets, but they are temporary measures that do not address fundamental weaknesses in the architecture of the EMU. The temporary measures, however, have provided European leaders with time to consider changes in the governance of the currency union. Reforms have also focused on developing more effective means of coordinating national fiscal policies and on promoting faster and more balanced growth. These are described briefly below.

Fiscal Policy Reforms

As discussed earlier, there have been efforts to reform the framework for European fiscal policy coordination and enforcement of European fiscal rules. On September 15, 2011, the EU Parliament approved new rules that provide a limited amount of additional power to EU authorities in controlling public debt levels of member countries.53 The rules strengthen the SGP by improving budgetary surveillance of Member countries. If Member countries continue to run excessive budget deficits, the EC would eventually be able to impose a fine of up 0.1% of GDP. Countries found to be falsifying their economic statistics could be subject to a fine of 0.2% of GDP.54

At the December 2011 Summit, leaders announced the creation of a new fiscal compact.55 The primary focus of the fiscal compact is an agreement that government budgets should be balanced or in surplus, and that constitutions should be amended to reflect this rule. The United Kingdom government was the only one of the 27 EU members not to sign on to the compact. At the Summit, the UK was unable to secure safeguards it desired regarding financial supervision and regulation, and therefore blocked the compact from taking the form of an amendment to the EU treaty.

Economic Growth Policies

Important for securing the long-term viability of the EMU is reversing several years of weak economic growth. Whatever fiscal reforms and surveillance targets are adopted, the Eurozone economies will find it very difficult to restore public finances and regain competitiveness in the absence of more rapid economic growth.56

Most economists predict that the Eurozone as whole will incur a minor contraction in 2012 (less than 1 percent) before it returns to modest growth in 2013. Growth is declining in large part because fiscal policy is highly contractionary across the Eurozone. Monetary policy, until the last quarter 2011, was also relatively restrictive, leaving only structural reforms to boost economic growth.57

For all Eurozone countries, the ECB and the European Commission have stressed the importance in their view of pressing forward with difficult structural reforms that have prevented the completion of the European common market. Removing remaining trade barriers, especially in the services sector, is viewed by the ECB and the EC as being particularly important for increasing growth. According to the ECB, only 20% of services provided in the EU have a crossborder dimension. A full implementation of the European Commission's services liberalization proposals could increase EU GDP growth rates by 0.6-1.5 percentage points.58 Other growth enhancing EU-wide reform efforts include promoting a common energy market and accelerating the implementation of new digital technologies in accordance with the objectives of the Europe 2020 growth strategy.

Addressing the trade imbalances within the Eurozone may also be important for achieving more rapid growth. To date the emphasis by the Eurozone leaders has been on dealing with the deficit countries by exhorting them to pay down debt, increase savings, and live within their means. While households and firms in deficit countries on the periphery have been spending less and saving more, there has been little offsetting increase in spending in the mostly northern surplus countries. With all members of the Eurozone simultaneously tryin to save more, aggregate demand is weakening further across the Eurozone and dampening economic growth.59

Possible Scenarios for the Future of the Eurozone

The current debt crisis has posed the most fundamental challenge to the Eurozone since the euro was introduced a decade ago and has led to speculation about the future of the Eurozone. Three scenarios have typically been discussed: (1) the crisis leads to a splintering or break-up of the Eurozone, with multiple members abandoning the euro; (2) the Eurozone survives the crisis largely intact; and (3) substantial reforms to the Eurozone architecture are implemented, leading to greater economic and political integration. Currently, the second scenario appears the most likely. European leaders are pursuing policy measures to keep the Eurozone intact; stepping up ECB liquidity support to private Eurozone banks, for example, appears to be stabilizing financial markets in the short-term. However, many analysts argue that longer-term policy changes under discussion, including introducing balanced budget amendments in nearly all EU member state constitutions, will not result in fundamental changes that address the structural problems inherent in the Eurozone and fall short of creating a full fiscal or political union.

Scenario 1. The Eurozone Breaks Apart

It was once considered unthinkable that countries would leave the Eurozone, but the current debt crisis has raised the possibility that one or more countries could exit the Eurozone. Exiting the Eurozone would entail countries abandoning the euro as their national currency, issuing a new national currency, and allowing the new national currency to appreciate or depreciate against the euro.

Exit by One or More Southern European Countries
The Eurozone could break apart if multiple Southern European countries decide to leave the Eurozone, or are pushed out of the Eurozone by Northern European countries. The biggest benefit to Southern European countries exiting the Eurozone would be new national currencies that are depreciated against the currency of its major trading partners in northern Europe (the euro). This

would help them regain competitiveness against the northern European countries, leading to an increase in exports and a decrease in imports. A surge in exports would spur economic growth, offsetting depressed demand at home due to austerity measures. Additionally, by increasing exports and lowering imports, Southern European countries would reduce their trade deficits and the borrowing needed to finance these deficits.

Exiting the Eurozone would involve potentially huge costs for the Southern European economies, however. First, the debt of Southern European countries is denominated in euros, and leaving the Eurozone in favor of a depreciated national currency could significantly raise the value of their debt in terms of national currency. Second, there are technical and legal obstacles to exiting the euro.60 Legislation would likely be required to issue the new national currency, and all contracts involving euros would have to be rewritten for the national currency. Numerous electronic machines involving euros, including computers, ATMs, and vending machines, would have to be reprogrammed or replaced, and new printing presses would be needed. Third, as investors and consumers anticipated that the new national currency would depreciate in value against the euro, massive capital flight from the country could trigger a major financial crisis in the country and put pressure on other vulnerable European countries. Such a financial crisis could have acute, negative impacts on short-term economic growth. Fourth, leaving the Eurozone would likely strain the country's political relations with other countries in the EU, and could possibly even lead to the country having to depart from the EU.

Exit by One or More Northern European Countries
Another variant of the Eurozone-breaking-apart scenario is exit by one or more Northern European countries due to frustration with the current debt crisis.61 When the Eurozone was created, there was concern among northern Eurozone members, particularly Germany, about the commitment of the ECB to price stability and the commitment of the Southern European countries to sustainable debt levels. Northern European countries did not want to be a "fiscal backstop" for the Southern European countries.62 To address these concerns, the ECB was created with the primary goal of price stability (compared, for example, to the

U.S. Federal Reserve, which has a dual mandate of price stability and full employment), the legal text establishing the euro included a "no bail-out" clause, and limits were put in place on the governments' overall outstanding debt levels (60% of GDP) and annual budget deficits (3% of GDP).

However, the current debt crisis has thrown these commitments into question. Some have argued that the ECB's decision to buy bonds of distressed Eurozone countries represents a loss of independence for the ECB, and political support in some of the Northern Eurozone countries for the financial assistance package for the vulnerable Eurozone countries has, at times, been ambivalent at best. Some have suggested that one or more Northern European countries could exit the Eurozone in favor of a new national currency. In Germany, four academics have, unsuccessfully, tried to challenge the constitutionality of Germany's membership in the Eurozone in German courts.63

Even if reverting to a new national currency could regain Northern European countries greater control over their monetary policy and reduce their financial commitments to the Southern European countries, leaving the Eurozone could be costly. A new national currency for one of the Northern European countries would likely appreciate against the euro, complicating the exportled growth strategies that several Northern European countries pursue. The Northern Eurozone countries would also face the same technical, legal, and political challenges to exiting the euro that face the Southern Eurozone countries, discussed above. However, some observers believe that banks in Northern European countries, even with new national currencies, could still accept debt payments in euros from Southern European countries without posing a risk to their solvency.64 This scenario would also have significant repercussions for the EU and the future of European integration.

Scenario 2. The Eurozone Survives

A second possible scenario is that the Eurozone emerges from the crisis largely in its current form. The status quo in the Eurozone could be maintained if market pressures on vulnerable

Southern European countries are calmed by the magnitude of the ECB liquidity support to Eurozone banks and bond purchases, financial support from the EFSF and the IMF, austerity packages in the Southern Eurozone countries, and an orderly restructuring of Greek bonds. Austerity and structural reforms could also successfully lower prices in Southern European countries, reducing imbalances within the Eurozone and obviating the need for additional integration of fiscal policies at the Eurozone level. The new institutional arrangements being proposed could increase integration among European countries, but fall short of a creating a full fiscal or political union.

Some have expressed concern that if the Eurozone does emerge from the crisis in its current form, the underlying problems with the architecture of the Eurozone that led to the current crisis would not be addressed. Failure to address these issues, including coordination of fiscal policies at the European level and correction of the imbalances within the Eurozone that developed over the past decade, may mean that similar crises lie ahead. The likelihood of this second scenario, that the Eurozone survives in its current form, largely depends on whether financial markets have confidence in the current crisis response measures. Specifically, much could depend on whether financial markets have confidence in the soundness of the reforms implemented or whether markets are left wondering if reforms will lead to more sustainable fiscal positions. In the fall of 2011, the crisis threatened to spread more broadly, but markets appear to be reassured by increased liquidity support by the ECB to Eurozone banks, announced in December 2011, and by the steps that Italy and Spain both took to curb deficits. However, it is unclear how long the ECB will be willing to provide this support, and how long these policy measures will reassure markets. The January 2012 downgrade by Standard & Poor's on the credit ratings of France, Italy, and seven other Eurozone countries underscored that more decisive and comprehensive responses from EU leaders could be required if the Eurozone is to continue to survive.

Scenario 3. The Eurozone Becomes More Integrated

A third possible scenario is that substantial reforms to the Eurozone architecture are implemented, leading to greater economic and political integration. This scenario would entail implementing reforms to reduce fiscal free-riding and to enhance the ability of the Eurozone to respond to future crises, if and when they arise. Greater fiscal federalism and a clear mechanism to provide emergency financial assistance to vulnerable countries would also be a goal. Several proposals, as discussed in the previous section, are currently being developed and are under consideration that are intended to accomplish these goals. Most concretely, European leaders have already taken steps to create a permanent fund to provide financial assistance to Eurozone members, the ECB has taken on new powers that increase its flexibility to respond to financial crises in the Eurozone, and the EU has passed new legislation that would introduce significant reforms to economic governance. As the crisis has continued, EU officials have pushed for more integration. In December 2011, some EU leaders pledged to pursue tighter fiscal coordination, including through balanced budget amendments.

However, fiscal policies are an important issue of national sovereignty, and it remains to be seen whether, or to what extent, national governments in the Eurozone will be willing to concede control over national budgets to European authorities or implement balanced budget amendments. Also, given the unpopularity of the financial assistance package for Greece and the broader support mechanisms for vulnerable Eurozone members with voters in Northern European countries, it is unclear whether countries will be willing to continue providing financial assistance to Eurozone members in crisis. Today, the EU budget represents about 1% of EU GDP and proposals to boost that by even 0.1% have consistently drawn vetoes from several EU members. Likewise, proposals to create EU-wide bonds ("Eurobonds") instead of bonds issued by national governments has been resisted by some EU members, most notably Germany. A recent German constitutional court decision that prohibits any future guarantees benefitting additional Eurozone members without the prior approval of the Bundestag may further constrain the German government from supporting the issuance of Eurobonds.65

While the likelihood of this third scenario—the Eurozone becomes more tightly integrated—has increased since the start of the crisis, it is by no means assured. As the crisis has unfolded, it has become clear that small, piecemeal steps by EU officials are not sufficient to calm markets about the crisis response. Given the public statements by EU leaders about the commitment to avoid countries leaving the Eurozone, it seems likely that more comprehensive response measures may be taken if the markets lose confidence in the current policy measures, or if the ECB becomes unwilling to intervene in markets. However, political obstacles to implementing measures that increase fiscal integration in meaningful ways remain formidable.

Implications for U.S. Interests

The Eurozone crisis can affect U.S. economic and political interests in important ways. A major U.S. concern is that a sovereign default by Greece or other Eurozone member or the failure of a major European financial institution could reverberate throughout the global economy in much the same way as the U.S. sub-prime crisis did in 2008. At a time when the U.S. economy is weak, another wave of credit freeze-ups and instability in the European banking sector could weaken U.S. financial institutions and nudge the U.S. economy into recession. Slower growth or a recession in the Eurozone could also adversely affect U.S exports and sales of U.S. companies operating in Europe and over time adversely affect U.S. GDP growth. While the Obama Administration, the Federal Reserve, and Congress have been engaged in monitoring and working towards an orderly resolution of the crisis, U.S. actions that could make a major difference are limited.

Economic Implications

The U.S. and Eurozone economies play major roles in the world economy and are crucially important for each other's prosperity. The two sides combined account for around 40% of world GDP,

25% of world trade, 60% of world foreign direct investment flows, and 60%-70% of world banking assets and financial services. They also remain each other's most important market for exports of goods and services, and are each other's primary source for foreign direct investment. U.S. companies operating in Europe and European companies operating in the United States employ up to 15 million workers on both sides of the Atlantic.66

Given these strong economic linkages, it is not surprising that the U.S. economy can be negatively impacted by the Eurozone crisis via both financial and trade linkages. Already there have been instances where concerns that the crisis is deepening have precipitated extreme volatility in U.S. stock prices. The unexpected resignation of an influential member of the ECB on September 9, 2011, for example, reportedly contributed to a 5% drop in European stock markets and a decline of more than 2% in major U.S. stock indexes.67

The debt problems of Greece, Ireland, Italy, Portugal, and Spain constitute a serious risk to the European banking system— particularly German, French, and British banks, which have close ties to U.S. banks. There are continuing concerns how these banks would be able to absorb losses on bonds should one of these countries default or restructure its debt. There are related concerns that should these banks' financial positions deteriorate or collapse, they would not be able to make payments owed to U.S. banks.

At the same time, the December 2011 decision by the ECB to provide European banks with large amounts of cheap credit for up to three years has eased concerns of any disorderly winding down of European bank holdings.68

In terms of international trade, the U.S. and Eurozone countries have one of the largest bilateral relationships in the world. If the Eurozone economy stagnates this year or slips into recession, demand for U.S. exports and the sales and profits of U.S. multinationals operating in Europe will be depressed. If the euro begins to depreciate more steeply against the dollar due to slower growth and loss of confidence in the euro, these adverse impacts on the U.S. economy could be amplified.69

A stronger dollar/weaker euro would also likely have some effects on U.S.-Eurozone foreign direct investment flows. Currently, Eurozone countries account for 26% of all U.S. direct investment abroad and for 44% of all foreign direct investment in the United States.70 Based on slower growth in Europe, U.S. investors may look towards emerging markets for additional investments, particularly since profits generated in euros would translate into fewer dollars, hurting the bottom line of U.S. parent companies. An offsetting factor could be that European stocks and assets with a weaker euro would look cheaper and more attractive, attracting U.S. capital to Europe.

Economists tend to be divided on the magnitude of any impacts on the U.S. economy. If the Eurozone economy contracts only modestly in 2012 (some forecasts are predicting a 0.2% drop in Eurozone GDP followed by a rebound to 1.0% growth in 2013) the impact on the U.S. economy is likely to be minimal.

However, the economic impact could be much more substantial if the Eurozone were to plunge into a deep and prolonged recession or even break-up due to a deepening sovereign debt crisis. By one estimate, a complete break-up of the Eurozone could lead to a 10% cumulative loss of output over the first two years.71 Combined with a likely adverse impact on the functioning of the EU's single market, U.S. exports of goods and services to Europe (which totaled over $300 billion in 2011) could be significantly reduced.

U.S. Policy Options

Measures that the Obama Administration could consider to help defuse the Eurozone crisis are limited. The most direct option involves the Federal Reserve Board, which has the authority to provide foreign central banks with an unlimited amount of dollars for an equivalent amount of currency. In 2007, 2008, and again in September 2011 the Fed did just this, swapping dollars for euros in order to provide the ECB with liquidity to calm capital markets. The Fed can also make short-term loans to commercial banks in distress in order to protect the U.S. financial system. Some in Congress have voiced opposition to these activities on the grounds that they constitute a "bailout" of European banks and governments.72

Beyond direct action by the Fed, the Obama Administration is left to exhorting European officials and U.S. financial institutions to do the right thing. Treasury Secretary Timothy Geithner, for example, has implored European officials to take more forceful actions to deal with the debt crisis.73 Alternatively, the administration could also encourage countries such as China and Saudi Arabia to help alleviate the crisis through additional purchases of European debt. Stable European financial markets and a growing world economy, it can be argued, are strongly in the interests of these countries as well as the United States.

Political Implications

Over the years, a key U.S. political interest has been a prosperous, peaceful, and stable Europe. In support of this interest, successive U.S. administrations have supported European efforts at economic and political integration. U.S. policy on the euro and the EMU has generally been that if it is good for Europe, it will be good for the United States. For example, on January 4, 1999, then President Clinton issued the following statement:74

We welcome the launch of the Euro, an historic step that 11 nations have taken toward a more complete Economic and Monetary Union (EMU). The United States has long advocated for European integration, and we admire the steady progress that Europe has demonstrated in taking the often difficult budget decisions that make this union possible. A strong and stable Europe, with open markets and robust growth, is good for America and good for the world. A successful economic union that contributes to a dynamic Europe is clearly in our long-term interests.

Given this history, if the Eurozone emerges from the crisis close to its present form or even stronger than before, strong U.S.-EU political ties are likely to continue. Only in the possible scenario of the Eurozone breaking apart are the effects likely to raise questions about the status quo. Major challenges to political ties could emerge if a break-up of the Eurozone were accompanied by growing divisions between key European countries, economic and social turmoil in selected countries, or a return to more nationalistic policies. The Obama Administration, like previous administrations, believes that a prosperous, secure, and increasingly integrated Europe that is capable of partnering with the United States in addressing mutual policy challenges is in the U.S. interest. On the other hand, it might also be argued that if a break-up were to occur, the United States might have greater influence with individual members of the EU. Those who held this view might also argue that a break-up could make the EU less of a rival to the United States.

Concluding Observations

The Eurozone crisis has highlighted cracks in the architecture of the currency union. Efforts to make the currency union more stable and sustainable in the long run represent one of the most fundamental challenges European leaders have faced in an over 50-year effort to advance political and economic integration. The U.S. stake in the outcome of these efforts, given the magnitude of U.S. economic and political ties with Europe, is considerable.

European proposals to date to reform the currency union center heavily on increasing fiscal coordination and integration in ways that do not surrender members' autonomy to make their own spending and tax decisions to a supra-EU entity. Rather, the proposals seek to strengthen current Stability and Growth Pact rules, partly through some form of sanctions, and to provide more policy coordination on budgets and other fiscal matters. Backed by the creation of liquidity facilities and the continued active involvement of the ECB in crisis management, European leaders have a limited period of time to calm financial markets and bolster confidence in the currency union. At the same time, the deepening crisis has prompted much stronger proposals such as the issuance of Eurobonds and a greater pooling of budgetary resources as a way to provide a stronger fiscal foundation for the monetary union.

Whether the currently contemplated reforms prove sufficient to ensure the sustainability and viability of the currency union is unclear. A number of factors and developments could either bolster or destabilize the currency union.

Factors and developments that could bolster the Eurozone include the following:

- Given that the EMU is largely a political undertaking and a major symbol of European integration, European leaders and elites may be highly motivated to keep the EMU intact.

- The proposals adopted to date introduce institutions and policies that represent somewhat higher levels of integration and commitment to budgetary discipline— elements that are considered necessary to rebuild market confidence in the euro for the future.
- The creation of the European Stability Mechanism (ESM) to replace the EFSF beginning in July 2012 provides a permanent facility to extend bridge loans to countries that are temporarily shut out of bond markets. In return, debtor countries have agreed to much stricter membership rules.
- The ECB has demonstrated willingness to help members in fiscal distress by buying their bonds on secondary markets, and it has acted to provide low-interest rate (one percent or less) loans to Eurozone banks for three years in order to ensure their financial stability.
- European and IMF rescue programs put into place for Greece, Ireland, and Portugal have been conditioned on fiscal and structural reforms of product and labor markets that are necessary to regain market confidence. Moreover, these reforms will improve the potential for economic growth and strengthen the euro in the long run.
- Steps taken to date have prevented contagion from spreading to Italy and Spain, countries deemed too large to bail-out.

Factors and possible developments that could weaken the sustainability of the currency union in its current form include the following:
- Solutions adopted to date may not may not keep a lid on bond yields. The result could make some sovereign defaults and bank failures unavoidable.
- There appears to be little political support for financing debt by issuing Eurobonds which would be guaranteed by all Eurozone members. In the longrun, mutualization of debt may be necessary to generate low risk-free

interest rates that will enable all Eurozone countries time to put their public finances on a stronger footing.

- The issuance of Eurobonds, in any case, may not prevent debt crises so long as the current account imbalances within the Eurozone persist. Such imbalances drain demand and employment from the deficit countries in the periphery, forcing these governments to run big deficits.
- Even with common bonds and stricter fiscal rules and targets, the public finances of the Eurozone may not improve markedly in the absence of more vigorous economic growth. Growth prospects, however, are poor as fiscal policy is highly contractionary across the Eurozone. Reforms to increase labor mobility and wage flexibility could boost growth, but these reforms make take years to come to fruition.
- The fundamental problem of countries at very different levels of development living with a single monetary policy and a single exchange rate will remain.

---

1 Germany was widely criticized, including by U.S. officials, for waiting several months after the onset of the Greek crisis in February 2010 before agreeing to loan facilities for Greece and other Eurozone member states. German reluctance is thought to have stemmed primarily from strong domestic opposition to the proposed relief packages. Many Germans consider Greece's problems to be a consequence of Greek government profligacy and, as such, see Greece as a burden on the German taxpayer. In light of this opposition, German Chancellor Merkel insisted that the Greek government commit to significant austerity measures before giving her support to a European assistance package. Nevertheless, the significant German public opposition to assisting Greece and establishing the loan facilities suggests that the German government could have a difficult time winning support for future monetary transfers to other Eurozone countries. This could present a significant challenge as European leaders engage in ongoing efforts to contain the crisis and shore up the banking sector.

2 The United States is the largest financial contributor to the IMF, and some Members of Congress have expressed reservations about the IMF loan to Greece. In response to the IMF loan to Greece, Congress included provisions in the financial regulatory legislation (P.L. 111-203) to protect IMF resources.

3 Implementation of the package is pending negotiations with Greece about meeting the imposed conditions. For elaboration and analysis of the Greek debt crisis, see CRS Report R41167, *Greece's Debt Crisis: Overview, Policy Responses, and Implications*, coordinated by Rebecca M. Nelson.

4 Statement by the Euro Area Heads of State or Government, December 9, 2011,

http://www.consilium.europa.eu.uedocs/cms_Dat/docs/pressdata/en/ec/1266 58.pdf.

5 Liz Alderman and Rachel Donadio, "Debt Ratings Cut for 9 Countries Amid Euro Woes," *New York Times,* January 14, 2012. The other countries downgraded were Austria, Slovenia, Slovakia, Spain, Malta, Cyprus, and Portugal.

6 Nelson D. Schwartz, "Euro Woes Could Revive Bout of Market Volatility," *New York Times,* January 16, 2012.

7 A total of 17 states (Austria, Belgium, Cyprus, Estonia, Finland, France, Germany, Greece, Ireland, Italy, Luxembourg, Malta, Netherlands, Portugal, Slovakia, Spain, and Slovenia) of the 27-member European Union (EU) participate in an economic and monetary union (EMU) with the euro as the single currency. The other members of the EU are Bulgaria, Czech Republic, Denmark, Hungary, Latvia, Lithuania, Poland, Romania, Sweden, and the United Kingdom. All 27 members take part in the "economic union" through various forms of policy coordination, a single market, and single external trade policy, but 17 members have taken economic integration a step further, to the EMU. Denmark and the United Kingdom were granted special opt-outs of the currency union and are legally exempt from joining unless their governments decide otherwise, either by parliamentary vote or referendum. Sweden has gained a *de-facto* opt-out through the use of various legal provisions. The other 7 members of the EU who joined after 2004 have committed or are expected to adopt the euro as soon as they meet certain economic policy targets.

8 Ben Hall and Quentin Peel, "Adrift Amid a Rift," *Financial Times,* June 24, 2010.

9 Jacob Funk Kirkegaard, "How Europe Can Muddle Through Its Crisis," *Peterson Institute for International Economics,* December 2010.

10 Neil Irwin and Michael Birnbaum, "Fed Move to Steer Dollars to Banks in the Euro Zone," *Washington Post,* September 16, 2011.

11 Senate Banking, Security and International Trade and Finance Subcommittee, September 22, 2011; House Financial Services, International Monetary Policy and Trade, October 25, 2011; Foreign Affairs, Europe, and Eurasia Subcommittee, October 27, 2011; Senate Foreign Relations, European Subcommittee, November 2, 2011; and House Oversight Subcommittee on TARP, Financial Services, and Bailouts of Public and Private Programs, December 15, 2011.

12 Conrad De Aenlle, "That Bright Light May Be Deceiving," *New York Times,* January 8, 2012.

13 For more information, see Harold James, *International Monetary Cooperation Since Breton Woods* (Oxford: Oxford University Press, 1996).

14 Katina Borsch, "Germany, The Euro and Politics of the Bail-out," *Centre for European Reform,* Briefing Note, June 2010.

15 For further background on the economic costs and benefits of monetary union with a focus on the EMU, see Paul De Grauwe, *Economics of Monetary Union* (Oxford: Oxford University Press, 2009).

16 World Bank's World Development Indicators database. Data in current US$.

17 World Bank's World Development Indicators database. Data in current US$.

18 For more on the bilateral economic relationship between the United States and the EU, see CRS Report RL30608, *EU-U.S. Economic Ties: Framework, Scope, and Magnitude,* by William H. Cooper.

19 Cost-in-freight data.

20 U.S. Department of Commerce, Bureau of Economic Analysis, http://www.bea.gov.

21 To participate in the initial formation of the EMU, each member had to meet the following five convergence criteria by 1998: (1) national legislation governing the country's financial system had to be compatible with the treaty provisions controlling the European System of Central Banks; (2) a rate of inflation within 1.5% of the rates in the three participating countries with the lowest rates; (3) reduction of its government deficits to below 3% of its gross national product; (4) currency exchange rates within the limits defined by the Exchange Rate Mechanism (ERM) (an intermediary step toward a single currency that attempted to stabilize exchange rates by fixing rates through variable bands) for at least two years; and (5)interest rates within 2% of the rates in the three participating countries with the lowest rates.

22 Paul De Grouse, *Economics of Monetary Union.*

23 Article 125 TFEU is often referred to as the EU's "no-bailout" clause. It states: The Union shall not be liable for or assume the commitments of central governments, regional, local or other public authorities, other bodies governed by public law, or public undertakings of any Member State, without prejudice to mutual financial guarantees for the joint execution of a specific project. A Member State shall not be liable for or assume the commitments of central governments, regional, local or other public authorities, other bodies governed by public law, or public undertakings of another Member State, without prejudice to mutual financial guarantees for the joint execution of a specific project.

24European leaders drew reference to these exceptions (Article 122(2) TFEU) in crafting new crisis management facilities. They explicitly based the bailout actions on the grounds that the debt crisis endangered the solvency of entire states and posed a serious threat to the euro and financial stability of the monetary union. For a contrary view that the euro was endangered by the crisis, see Hans-Werner Sinn, "Rescuing Europe," *CWSifo Forum*, Volume 1, August 2010. Sinn argues that the bailout was engineered primarily to protect French, and to a lesser extent, German banks.

25 The Protocol on Excessive Deficit Procedure established a mechanism for countries to meet the specific guidelines that are applied under Article 104 of the Maastricht Treaty. Under this protocol, EU members are expected to have an annual budget deficit no greater than 3% of GDP at market prices and government debt no more than an amount equivalent to 60% of GDP.

26 The Stability and Growth Pact (SGP) is an agreement by European Union members to conduct their fiscal policy in a manner that facilitates and maintains the EMU. The Pact is based on Articles 99 and 104 of the Maastricht Treaty, and related decisions. It consists of (1) a political commitment by all parties involved in the SGP to the full and timely implementation of the budget surveillance process; (2) regular surveillance aimed at preventing budget deficits from going above the 3% reference value; and (3) corrective elements which require member states to take immediate action when the 3% reference value is breached or face the imposition of sanctions.

27 Beetsma, Roel M.W.J., and Xavier Debrun, *Implementing the Stability and Growth Pact: Enforcement and Procedural Flexibility*, IMF Working Paper WP/05/59, International Monetary Fund, March 2005.

28 Martin Feldstein, "The Euro's Fundamental Flaws," *The International Economy,* Spring 2010, p. 11.

29 Faltin, Dirk, and Katherine Klingensmith, "Eurozone Economics: The Future of the Euro in Jeopardy," *UBS Wealth Management Research,* July 13, 2010.

30Martin Feldstein, p.12.

31 Bank for International Settlements (BIS), "Consolidated International Claims of BIS Reporting Banks," Publication data up to 2009Q4, June 2010, Table 9B: Consolidated Foreign Claims of Reporting Banks - Immediate Borrower Basis,

http://www.bis.org/statistics/consstats.htm. Data includes exposure to the GIIPS governments (sovereigns) and private sectors.

32 Gilles Saint-Paul, "Is the Euro a Failure?," *VoxEU,* May 5, 2010.

33 Uri Dadush and Bennett Stancil, "Europe's Debt Crisis: More than a Fiscal Problem," in *Paradigm Lost: The Euro in Crisis,* ed. Uri Dadush and Contributors (Carnegie Endowment for International Peace, 2010), pp. 9-15.

34 The current account is the sum of the balance of trade (exports minus imports of goods and services), net factor income such as interest payments and dividends, and net transfer payments such as foreign aid. Measures to reduce a current account deficit usually involve increasing exports or decreasing imports. Economists tend to argue that this can be accomplished most effectively by increasing domestic savings or reducing borrowing of households and government.

35 Dirk Faltin and Katherine Klingensmith, "Eurozone Economics: The Future of the Euro in Jeopardy," p. 6.

36 Given that about 75% of all Eurozone trade constitutes exports of one Eurozone member to another (so-called "intra- Eurozone trade"), the trade surpluses of one Eurozone country or group of countries are to a large extent matched by the deficits of others.

37 Gilles Saint-Paul, "Is the Euro a Failure?", *VoxEU,* May 5, 2010.

38 Dick Faltin and Katherine Klingensmith, "Eurozone Economics: The Future of the Euro In Jeopardy," p.5.

39 Ibid., p. 8.

40 For more information, see: CRS Report R41167, *Greece's Debt Crisis: Overview, Policy Responses, and Implications,* coordinated by Rebecca M. Nelson.

41 For more information, see: CRS Report R41838, *Sovereign Debt in Advanced Economies: Overview and Issues for Congress,* by Rebecca M. Nelson.

42 Art Patnaude and Mark Brown, "European Funding Costs Hit Record Highs," *Wall Street Journal,* September 12, 2011.

43 At the December 2011 Summit, leaders extended €200 billion (about $260 billion) in bilateral lines of credit from European countries to the IMF, leaving open the possibility that other countries outside of Europe could also contribute to the IMF.

44 The current balance of payments facility was created under Article 143 of the Lisbon Treaty, which limits assistance to "member states with a derogation," i.e., those outside the Eurozone.

45 Council Regulation (EU) No. 407/2010 of 11 May 2010 establishing a European financial stabilization mechanism. Official Journal of the European Union, December 5, 2010. L 118/1.

46 Council of the European Union, Press Release, Extraordinary Council Meeting, Economic and Financial Affairs, Brussels, May 9/10, 2010.

47 Joshua Chaffin and Quentin Peel, "Eurozone Bail-out Fund Hit by Downgrade," *Financial Times*, January 17, 2012.

48 Willem Buiter, *Global Economics View, Europe: Fear and Panic Make Poor Counsellors*, Citgroup, August 12, 2011.

49 David Oakley, Peter Garnham, and Ralph Atkin, "ECB reveals €16.5bn bond purchases," *Financial Times*, May 17, 2010.

50 Reuters, "ECB's spent 14 bln euros on bonds ahead of Stark exit," September 12, 2011.

51 David McHugh, "Europe's Banks Jump at $639B in ECB loans," USA Today, December 22, 2011.

52 In response to the beginnings of the recent financial crisis, similar swap lines were established in December 2007 and expired in February 2010. On the re-establishment of these lines, see Federal Reserve, "Federal Reserve, European Central Bank, Bank of Canada, Bank of England, and Swiss National Bank Announce Reestablishment of Temporary U.S. Dollar Liquidity Swap Facilities.,"

53 Claire Davenport, "EU Wins Battle Over National Debt Vetting," *Euractiv.com*, September 15, 2011.

54 Honor Mahoney, "Deal Reached on EU Economic Governance Laws," *euobserver.com*, September 15, 2011.

55 The fiscal compact is still a "proposed" compact. The language is being drafted, the content debated, and it will have to be ratified by all members.

56 Simon Tilford and Philip Whyte, "Why Stricter Rules Threaten the Eurozone," Centre for European Reform, October 2011.

57 Many Eurozone policymakers argue that fiscal austerity, even if pursued by all member states simultaneously, will not be contractionary because it will boost consumer and business confidence that government finances are sustainable. Over time, it is argued that consumption and investment will grow along with the rising confidence.

58 Lorenzo Bini Smaghi, *Imbalances and Sustainability in the Euro Area*, European Central Bank, Presentation at the ECB and its Watchers Conference, Frankfurt, July 9, 2010.

59 Simon Tilford and Philip Whyte, "Why Stricter Rules Threaten the Eurozone," p.24.

60 Barry Eichengreen, "The Euro: Love It or Leave It?," *VoxEU*, November 17, 2007, http://www.voxeu.org/index.php?q=node/729.

61 Gerard Baker, "Will Germany Leave the Euro?," *The Spectator*, June 19, 2010, pp. 14-15.

62 Ibid.

63 Wolgang Proissi, "Why Germany Fell Out of Love with Europe," *Brueghel Essay and Lecture Series*, July 2020, pp.15-17.

64At the same time, the value of Northern banks' euro-denominated assets would still fall relative to their liabilities denominated in new currency.

65 George Soros, "Does the Euro Have A Future?" *The New York Review of Books*, October 13, 2011.

66 CRS Report R41553, *International Trade and Finance: Key Policy Issues for the 112th Congress*, coordinated by Raymond J. Ahearn, *The Transatlantic Economy 2011*, Johns Hopkins Center for Transatlantic Relations, 2011.

67 Jack Ewing and Nicholas Lulish, "A Setback for the Euro Zone: Central Bank Resignation Reveals a Widening Split on the Debt Crisis," *New York Times,* September 10, 2011.

68 Steven Mufson, "Ailing EU banks could hamper U.S.," *New York Times,* December 23, 2011.

69 Given that a variety of factors such as relative growth rates, differential interest rates, and perceptions of stability can affect exchange rates, predictions of movements in the dollar/euro rate are difficult to make. During 2011 the euro depreciated or weakened against the dollar by about 3 percent.

70 U.S. Department of Commerce, *Survey of Current Business,* various editions.

71 ING Global Economics, "EMU Break-up: Quantifying the Unthinkable," July 7, 2010.

72 Bruce Stokes, "Above the Fray No More," *National Journal,* May 21, 2011.

73 John Fraher and Ian Katz, "Geithner to Prod EU on Crisis Fight, *Washington Post,* September 14, 2011.

74 Website: http://clinton6.nara.gov/1999/01/1999-01-04-statement-by-the-president-on-the-launch-of-the-euro.html

CRS Report for Congress
Prepared for Members and Committees of Congress
January 17, 2012

The Outlook for the Euro Crisis and Implications for the U.S.

By
C. Fred Bergsten
Director, Peterson Institute for International Economics

Doom and gloom about the euro abounds. An increasing number of commentators and economists have begun to question whether the common currency can survive.

The economic and financial problems in the euro area are clearly serious and plentiful. The area is in the midst of multiple, frequently overlapping, and mutually reinforcing crises. A fiscal crisis is centered on Greece but visible across the southern euro area and Ireland. A competitiveness crisis is manifest in large and persistent current account deficits in the euro area periphery and even larger current account imbalances. A banking crisis was first evident in Ireland but has now spread throughout the area via accelerating concerns over sovereign solvencies.

I believe that these fears are vastly overblown. The European crisis is political, and even largely presentational, which is key to understanding how the crisis has developed and how it will be resolved.

The lack of confidence in the euro is first and foremost rooted in a crisis of fundamental institutional design. The Economic and Monetary Union (EMU) adopted in the 1990s comprised an extensive (though still incomplete) monetary union, with the euro and the European Central Bank (ECB). But it included virtually no economic union: no fiscal union, no economic governance institutions, and no meaningful coordination of structural economic policies.

It was assumed by the architects that economic union would inexorably follow monetary union. However, there was no pressure to create an economic union during the expansion period prior to the Great Recession. When the crisis hit, the contradiction triggered severe market reactions that continue to this day.

There are only two alternatives. Europe can jettison the monetary union. Or it can adopt a complementary economic union. For all the turmoil, Europe is well on its way to completing the original concept of a comprehensive economic and monetary union and that Europe will indeed emerge from the crisis much stronger as a result.

The key to understanding the evolution of the euro crisis is to observe and analyze what the Europeans do rather than what they say. They have resolved all of the many crises that have threatened the European integration project, throughout its history of more than half a century, in ways that strengthened the institution and moved the project forward. At each key stage of the current crisis, they have in fact done whatever is necessary to avoid collapse. In the crunch, both Germany and the ECB will pay whatever is necessary to avert disaster. The politics of each, as described below, assure this result.

The problem for the markets is that these central players cannot say that this is what they will do. There are two reasons. First, a commitment to bailouts without limit would represent the ultimate in moral hazard. It would relieve the debtor countries of the pressure necessary to compel them to take tough political decisions and maintain effective adjustment policies. Second, each of the four main classes of creditors—Germany and the other northern European governments, the ECB, private sector lenders, and the International Monetary Fund (as a conduit for non-EU governments like China)—will naturally try to transfer as many of the financial losses on Greek government bonds or European banks as possible onto the other three, limiting their own costs and risks in the process.

Every policymaker in Europe knows that the collapse of the euro would be a political and economic disaster for all and thus totally unacceptable. Fortunately, Europe is an affluent region with ample resources to solve its crisis—it is a matter of mobilizing the political will to pay rather than the economic ability to pay. Europe's key political actors in Berlin, Frankfurt, Paris, Rome, Athens, and elsewhere will thus quite rationally exhaust all alternative options in searching for the best possible deal but at the last minute come to an agreement.

This is a messy and indeed cacophonous process that is understandably unsettling to markets and inherently produces enormous instability. Miscalculation, and thus disaster, is always possible under such a scenario. But the process in fact relies on financial market volatility to incentivize solutions that will ultimately resolve the crisis. Europe's overriding political imperative to preserve the integration project will surely drive its leaders to ultimately secure the euro and restore the economic health of the continent.

The European Integration Project

The entire European project was of course driven by the existential geopolitical goal of halting the intra-European carnage that had persisted for at least a millennium and reached its murderous zenith in the first half of the 20th century. The postwar European leadership, driven primarily by Germany and France, chose the policy instrument of economic integration "to make future wars impossible." The project has experienced repeated severe crises over its initial half century but each was overcome, indeed giving way to renewed forward momentum for Europe as a whole. The overriding security imperative drove successive generations of political leaders to subordinate their national sovereign interests to the greater good of maintaining, and in fact extending, the European project.

Germany also has an overwhelming economic interest in the survival, and indeed strengthening, of the Eurozone. Its entire economic model is based on export-led growth and world-class international competitiveness. Before the euro, however, its large trade surpluses would often lead to sharp appreciation in the exchange rate of its national currency, the Deutsche Mark, that would to an important degree dampen its competitiveness and thus its growth.

Now, however, Germany enjoys the best of all worlds: the largest trade surplus of any country (even China) and a weak currency, as the euro reflects the much weaker economies of the periphery (and even France) as well as muscular Germany. Every German realizes that this unusual juxtaposition explains much of his country's ability to prosper through the Great Recession, and the current European phase thereof, that has severely retarded growth and job creation in almost every other country in Europe. They thus realize that it is imperative, in purely economic and financial terms of the national interest, to pay any conceivable price to hold the euro together.

The concept of a common currency was always an element in the region's vision of the ultimate goals of the integration project. Concrete thinking about an economic and monetary union in Europe goes back to 1970, when the *Werner Report*2 laid out a detailed three-stage plan for the establishment of EMU by 1980. Members of the European Community would gradually increase coordination of economic and fiscal policies while reducing exchange-rate fluctuations and finally fixing their currencies irrevocably. The collapse of the Bretton Woods system and the first oil crisis in the early 1970s, however, caused the *Werner Report* proposals to be set aside for a time.

By the mid-1980s, following the creation of the European Monetary System in 1979 and the initiation of Europe's internal market, European policymakers again took up the idea of an economic and monetary union. The *Delors Report* from 1989 envisioned the achievement of EMU by 1999, moving gradually (in three stages) towards closer economic coordination among the EU members with binding constraints on member states' national budgets and a single currency managed by an independent European Central Bank (ECB).

Optimal Currency Area (OCA) theory prescribes the characteristics required for a geographic area to obtain maximum economic benefits from adopting the same currency. It can offer guidance to economically rational leaders about whether it makes sense for their country to join a common currency. But it was not a carefully considered and detailed economic analysis that ultimately led to the creation of the euro. It was geopolitics and the completely unforeseen shock of German reunification in October 1990 that provided the political impetus for the creation of the Maastricht Treaty, which in 1992 laid the legal foundation and detailed design for today's euro area.

With the historical parity in Europe between (West) Germany and France no longer a political and economic reality, after German reunification, French president Francois Mitterrand and German Chancellor Helmut Kohl intensified the EMU process as a political project to complete the integration of the French,

German, and other European economies in an economic and monetary union that would accomplish full and irrevocable European unity.

This political imperative for launching the euro by 1999 frequently required that politically necessary compromises, rather than theoretically unambiguous rules, make up the institutional framework for the euro. OCA theory, and the earlier Werner and Delors reports discussing the design of EMU, had been explicit about the requirement to complement a European monetary union with a European economic union complete with binding constraints on member states' behavior. Political realities in Europe, however, made this goal unattainable within the time frame dictated by political leaders following German reunification.

The divergence in the economic starting points among the politically prerequisite "founding members" of the euro area made the imposition of firm fiscal criteria for membership in the euro area politically infeasible. The Maastricht Treaty in principle included at least two hard convergence criteria for euro area membership—a 3 percent limit on general government annual deficits and 60 percent limit on general government gross debt limit.6 However, in reality, these threshold values were anything but fixed as the Maastricht Treaty Article 104c stated that countries could exceed the 3 percent deficit target if "the ratio has declined substantially and continuously and reached a level that comes close to the reference value" or "excess over the reference value is only exceptional and temporary and the ratio remains close to the reference value." Euro area countries could similarly exceed the 60 percent gross debt target provided that "the ratio is sufficiently diminishing and approaching the reference value at a satisfactory pace."

The actual numerical reference values to article 104c of the Maastricht Treaty are in a protocol on the Excessive Deficit Procedure to the treaty. The Maastricht Convergence Criteria for euro area membership eligibility included three other metrics: inflation (within 1.5 percent of the three EU countries with the lowest inflation rate), long-term interest rates (within 2 percent of the three lowest interest rates in the European Union), and exchange-rate fluctuations (participation for two years in the ERM II narrow band of exchange-rate fluctuations).

In other words, it was a wholly political decision whether a country could become a member of the euro area or not.

Membership was not objectively determined by the fundamental economic strengths and reform record of the country in question. And it was politically inconceivable to launch the euro without Italy, the third largest economy in continental Europe, or Belgium, home of the European capital Brussels. Hence both countries became members despite having gross debt levels of almost twice the Maastricht Treaty reference value of 60 percent in 1997-98.

As a result, Europe's monetary union was launched in 1999 with a set of countries that were far more diverse in their economic fundamentals, and far less economically integrated, than had been envisioned in the earlier Werner and Delors reports or would be dictated by OCA theories. Moreover, shortly after the launch of the euro, European political leaders further undermined the credibility of the rules-based framework for the coordination of national fiscal policies in the euro area. Building on the euro area convergence criteria, the Stability and Growth Pact (SGP) was intended to safeguard sound public finances, prevent individual euro area members from running unsustainable fiscal policies, and thus guard against moral hazard by enforcing budget discipline. However, faced with breaching the 3 percent deficit limit in 2002-04, France and Germany pushed through a watering down of the SGP rules in March 20057 that, as in the Maastricht Treaty, introduced sufficient flexibility into the interpretation of SGP that its enforcement became wholly political and with only limited reference to objective economic criteria and data.

In sum, the euro area by 2005 was, as a result of numerous shortcuts taken to achieve and sustain a political goal, a common currency area consisting of a very dissimilar set of countries without a central fiscal authority, without any credible enforcement of budget discipline, and without any real deepening of economic convergence.

Initially, however, none of these fundamental design flaws mattered. The financing costs in private financial markets of all euro area members quickly fell towards the traditionally low interest rates of Germany.

It is beyond the scope of this policy brief to interpret the causes of this colossal and sustained mispricing of credit risk in the euro area sovereign debt markets by private investors in the first years after the introduction of the euro. But the financial effects were obvious: Euro area governments and private investors were able to finance themselves at historically low (often significantly negative real) interest rates seemingly irrespective of their economic fundamentals.

Valéry Giscard d'Estaing, when he was finance minister of France, criticized the "exorbitant privilege" enjoyed by the United States as the issuer of the world's reserve currency, enabling it to pay for imports (and foreign investments) in its own currency and making it seemingly oblivious to balance of payment constraints. With sudden access to "German interest rates," many new euro area members suddenly enjoyed their own supercharged "exorbitant privilege." Large public and private debt overhangs were correspondingly built up in the euro area in the first years of the new currency and in the run-up to the global financial crisis in 2008.

European policymakers' initial denial and self-congratulations, coupled with financial markets' failure to properly assess the riskiness of different euro area countries and tendency to ignore the common currency's design flaws, thus conspired to ensure that the euro area, when it was finally struck by its first serious financial crisis in 2008-09, was hit by a double whammy of huge pre-crisis public and private debt overhangs and a faulty institutional design that prevented an expeditious solution that would be credible to those same markets.

The Political Battle to Save the Euro

During its first decade, the euro area institutional framework was that of a "fair weather currency." The area entered the Great Recession woefully under-institutionalized as a common currency flying on just one engine—the ECB—but without the unified fiscal entity that traditionally plays a critical role in combating large financial crises. The euro area leaders have had to build their crisis-fighting capacity and bailout institutions (the European Financial Stability Facility/European Stability Mechanism (EFSF/ESM)) from scratch, and in the midst of crisis, to prevent their immediate financial predicament from getting out of control while simultaneously reforming the flawed foundational institutions of the area. Achieving the dual policy goals of solving a current crisis while trying also to prevent the next one—and using the same policy tools to do both—is rarely easy.

This marks a crucial difference from the United States. Once the Troubled Asset Relief Program (TARP) was finally passed, close collaboration between the multiple existing institutions in the United States (Treasury, Federal Reserve, Federal Deposit Insurance Corporation) ultimately restored market confidence and stabilized the situation in March 2009. In the United States in 2008 – 09, the economic crisis compelled the Fed to immediately apply the so-called Powell Doctrine—overwhelming firepower—to restore shaken market confidence and give the federal government time to formulate a longer-term response in fits and starts through the TARP. This is a fairly well established crisis response function. The central bank comes out with monetary guns blazing and then sits back and prays that the politicians do the right thing. (Congress did of course pass TARP after initially rejecting it but has not yet chosen to institute a sustainable fiscal response for the United States.)

The ECB, as the only euro area institution capable of affecting financial markets in real time, is a uniquely powerful central bank. Its institutional independence is enshrined in the EU treaty and it is not answerable to any individual government. This has enabled it to function as a fully independent political actor, interacting with elected officials during the crisis in a manner inconceivable among its peers. Quite unlike normal central banks, which always have to worry about losing their institutional independence, in this crisis the ECB has been able to issue direct political demands to euro area leaders—as with the reform ultimatum conveyed to Silvio Berlusconi last August—and demand that they take action accordingly.

On the other hand, the ECB has not had the luxury of adopting the straightforward crisis tactics of the Federal Reserve and the US government within a fixed set of national institutions. The ECB cannot perform a "bridge function" until the proper authorities take over because no euro area fiscal entity exists. Moreover, to commit to a major "bridging monetary stimulus," as some have called for, would undermine chances of a permanent political resolution to the euro area's underlying under-institutionalization problem. Were the ECB to cap governments' financing costs at no more than 5 percent, for instance, euro area politicians would probably never make the painful but essential decisions.

Saddled with administering a common currency, and endowed with governing institutions flawed by early political compromises, it is hardly surprising that the ECB's dominant concern as it manages this crisis has been to prevent "political moral hazard" and not let euro area leaders off the hook. Precisely because Silvio Berlusconi would still be prime minister of Italy if the ECB had purchased unlimited amounts of Italian government bonds at an earlier time, the central bank is highly unlikely to provide the necessary assistance to euro area elected leaders to end the crisis—including the Italian successors of Silvio Berlusconi—unless and until they offer and implement a suitable quid pro quo.

It is imperative to understand that it is not the primary purpose of the ECB, as a political actor, to end market anxieties and thus the euro area crisis as soon as possible. It is instead focused on achieving its priority goals of getting government leaders to fundamentally reform the euro area institutions and structurally overhaul many euro area economies. Frankfurt cannot directly compel democratically elected European leaders to comply with its wishes but it can refuse to implement a "crisis bazooka" and thereby permit the euro area crisis to continue to put pressure on them to act. A famous American politician has said that "no crisis should be wasted" and the ECB is implementing such a strategy resolutely.

So far the ECB has been reasonably effective in this strategic bargaining with euro area governments. It has also consistently been willing to reverse itself when circumstances demanded. The initial Greek crisis in May 2010 led to the first "grand bargain" between the ECB (which agreed to set up the bond purchasing Securities Market Program) and euro area governments. Their agreement produced strong commitments for structural reforms in Spain and elsewhere. It also produced €440 billion in resources for the newly created EFSF, which proved to be an effective euro area fiscal agent when the problem was Greece, Ireland, and Portugal. Again, one must watch what they do rather than solely what they say.

The EFSF is inadequate when the problem becomes Italy and Spain, however. The ECB and euro area governments have therefore for some time been engaged in a new round of strategic bargaining to put together a sufficiently large financial rescue package, secure structural reform of the two big debtors (especially Italy) and, perhaps most importantly, to complete the euro area institutional house. The EU Summit on December 9, 2011 represented the latest round in this game of political poker.

The December 2011 Summit

The real economy in the euro area has gradually deteriorated as regional policymakers dithered in their management of the complex crisis. This rising "economic collateral damage" has increased the pressure to act and led many to speculate that the euro is facing collapse.

This is nonsense. It is abundantly evident that all the key political decision makers in Europe—the ECB, the German government, the French government, Italy, and even Greece—are keenly aware of the catastrophic costs of such an outcome. Greek politicians know that, without the euro and outside the European Union, their country would collapse into a politically vulnerable economic wasteland and/or experience a military coup (the collapse would be far worse than the economic crisis seen since 2009). Angela Merkel knows that, were the euro to collapse, Germany's banks would collapse too under the weight of their losses on loans to the euro-area periphery; the new Deutsche mark would skyrocket, undermining the entire German export economy; and Germany would once again be blamed for destroying Europe. The ECB of course would not want to put itself out of business.

Those political games of chicken are repeatedly being played by all actors to try to extract the best possible deal for themselves. In the end, all will compromise. It is not a coincidence that Greek political leaders, once threatened with expulsion from the euro by Angela Merkel and Nicolas Sarkozy at the G-20 meeting in Cannes, formed the previously elusive national unity government in one week. Italy moved in the same manner within days of its *diktat* from the ECB. Once Germany and the ECB feel they have gotten the best possible deal, or have run out of alternatives, they will pay whatever it takes to hold the euro together. Neither can afford not to. But neither can say so in advance or, at the other extreme, risk seeing their bluff called.

Seen through these lenses, the EU Summit on December 9, 2011 developed in an understandable and promising manner. Two issues were central.

First, after 18 months of accelerating economic crisis, EU leaders finally began detailed political discussions about how to reform the flawed euro area institutions. At German (and implicitly ECB) insistence, the talks focused on a new "fiscal compact" aimed at finally producing for the euro area a set of binding budget rules that will constrain member states' policy in the future. Due to the reluctance of the United Kingdom to accept a revision of the existing EU treaty, a new intergovernmental "coalition of the willing" compact may have to be negotiated among a sub-group of the 27 members of the European Union. Substantial legal and institutional uncertainty and "implementation risk" consequently surround these preliminary political decisions and the crucial legal details remain unfinalized. Yet the fact that 26 (or even 23) European heads of state and government declared their political intention to enter into a new fiscal compact, which will severely constrain their future fiscal sovereignty, is testament to the unflinching will to do whatever it takes to save the euro.

Many were disappointed by this narrow agenda and the lack of discussion of a larger centralized EU budget, like in the United States, or the immediate creation of joint eurobonds. However, it must be recalled that, as discussed earlier, Europe does not have the democratic legitimacy to collect taxes for a centralized budget at this point. Similarly, Europe lacks the compelling "endured in a common cause" (i.e., the Revolutionary War) political narrative that enabled Alexander Hamilton to pool together the debts of individual US states into common Treasury bills and bonds. Italy's debts have been run up to benefit Italians and other European taxpayers will surely revolt if suddenly compelled to pay part of them.

The reality in the euro area is that, for the foreseeable future and unlike in the United States, the overwhelming majority of government taxation and spending will continue to reside at the member state level for reasons of political legitimacy. Only a minor part will be pooled at the supra-national level. Restricting this spending via a new fiscal compact is consequently the only pragmatic route for now, leaving other aspects of euro area fiscal integration to the future.

Second, EU leaders tried to thrash out a sufficiently large financial firewall to restore confidence in the solvency of Italy and Spain. This issue was addressed in several ways. For one, euro area leaders reversed their initial intent to insert Private Sector Involvement (PSI) clauses into the new permanent ESM treaty. This should make it clear that private sovereign bond market investors face the same legal environment in the euro area as elsewhere, making the case for "Greece being a unique case" legally and politically more credible. This should ultimately help restore fleeting investor confidence in euro area sovereign bonds. In the grand game of distributing the costs of the euro area bailouts, private investors will not be asked to take haircuts other than in Greece in the hope they will then lend new money to the other debtor countries as the latter undertake the needed adjustments.

The Role of the International Monetary Fund

EU leaders further continued their sparring about the ultimate distribution of the costs of extending the euro area financial rescue by pledging €200 billion (€150 billion from the euro area) in new general resources to the International Monetary Fund (IMF). This would come in the form of loans from EU central banks8 with the political understanding that the resources would be utilized predominantly to stabilize Italy and Spain. This attempt to involve the IMF directly in the rescue of the two larger euro area economies is in many ways reminiscent of the two-thirds/one-third financing split between the euro area and the rest of the world (as shareholders of the IMF9) for the existing IMF programs for Greece, Ireland, and Portugal.

8. Note that this means that any loans made to the IMF by euro area central banks will expand the consolidated European System of Central Banks' (ESCB) balance sheet, even if the loans are not disbursed by the ECB itself.

9. The two-thirds/one-third breakdown is not entirely accurate, as the euro area members are sizable shareholders of the IMF themselves and hence in total contribute more than two-thirds of the total financing of these programs.

10. One might arguably also add the two ECB-covered bond purchase programs (~€62 billion) with unlimited liquidity of less than a three-year duration to these central bank support measures.

However, given the better economic fundamentals in Italy and Spain and the prohibitively high costs of extending to them the type of traditional IMF programs granted to the three smaller euro area economies, a less politically intrusive and less expensive vehicle for IMF involvement may be found. This will still presumably entail special IMF borrowing from surplus and creditor countries around the world. A number have already said they will participate in such an initiative: Brazil, new G-20 chair Mexico, Russia, and a number of non-euro Europeans. China and other large Asian holders of foreign exchange have been more coy. They have also clearly indicated a desire to diversify their huge reserves away from dollars, however, so new claims on the IMF would presumably look quite attractive to them from a purely financial management point of view.

Total IMF borrowing, and the creation of a "firewall" to insure against default by major euro area countries, should and probably will exceed €1 trillion. Taken in combination with the €500 billion in the EFSF/ESM, the €700 billion or more from the ECB from its previous programs (€211 billion in sovereign bond purchases through the Securities Markets Programme (SMP), €489 billion in three-year loans10), and its essentially unlimited liquidity provisions to the euro area banking system, this amount should convince even the most skeptical market participants that the "firewall" is adequate even for Italy and Spain.

In now turning to the IMF, the euro area leaders acknowledge that their previous "euro area governments only" EFSF bailout vehicle will not be an efficient mechanism through which to provide assistance to Italy and Spain. While this may seem like a political setback, going through the IMF rather than the (leveraged) EFSF in fact provides the euro area with significant credit enhancement because it makes it much more likely that other IMF member governments, e.g., China and other surplus countries, will choose to contribute.

In that way the IMF will quite likely serve as a far better leverage mechanism for the euro area's own resources (€150 billion) than had this money instead simply been added to the EFSF itself.11 Euro area governments will have successfully shifted part of the costs of any future financial rescues onto the rest of the world. The rest of the world will of course extract a suitable price from the euro area for this service in the form of European political concessions in other policy areas. This could, for instance, be a good time to demand that the euro area consolidate its representation on the IMF board to a single seat (from its current eight) and accelerate the transfer of its quota shares to the financially contributing emerging markets.

Routing euro area central bank loans through the IMF general resources also provides governments a better "legal fig-leaf" against political charges of "monetary financing" (voiced by, for instance, the German Bundesbank) than if such loans had been used to leverage the EFSF directly.

MOVING TOWARD FISCAL UNION

Recent ECB policies have similarly tried to shift the bailout cost to other entities. In his December 1, 2011 testimony before the EU Parliament Mario Draghi famously stated "We might be asked whether a new fiscal compact would be enough to stabilize markets and how a credible longer term vision can be helpful in the short term. Our answer is that it is definitely the most important element to start restoring credibility. Other elements might follow, but the sequencing matters."

This was immediately taken by markets to mean that, provided EU leaders agree on a new "fiscal compact," the ECB would be willing to step up its sovereign bond market interventions and largely pick up the tab for bailing out Italy and Spain.

Unsurprisingly, euro area bond markets rallied strongly in the expectation of an official sector bailout from the ECB until the next Mario Draghi press conference on December 8, 2011, when he walked back his earlier comments by stating in response to a question that: "The purpose of the SMP is to reactivate the transmission channels of monetary policy. The SMP is neither eternal nor infinite. We must keep this in mind and we do not want to circumvent Article 123 of the treaty, which prohibits the monetary financing of governments... the need to respect the spirit of the treaty should always be present in our minds." Hence the ECB would not be willing to proactively bail out private investors in the Italian and Spanish debt markets. Those markets fell dramatically on the very day of the EU Summit.

The ECB signal thus sent to EU leaders ahead of their summit seemed unambiguous: It is up to the fiscal authorities, not the monetary authorities, to pay to restore market confidence in the Italian and Spanish bond markets. By turning to the IMF at their summit, euro area leaders indicated that they had clearly gotten the message.

The ECB refused to intervene directly and more forcefully in the euro area sovereign bond markets on December 8, 2011. But the central bank did effectively bail out the entire EU banking system, and with it many of the private sovereign bond creditors, through a series of additional enhanced credit support measures to support bank lending and liquidity in the euro area. These included unlimited liquidity provisions for three years, compared to a previous maximum of one year, expanded ECB collateral eligibility to include bank loans, and cutting the reserve ratio in half to 1 percent.

These forceful ECB liquidity measures were clearly warranted given the stress in the inter-bank credit markets in the euro area. However, they also provide a potential back door for euro area banks to use some of the funding available from the ECB to purchase additional euro area sovereign bonds and thereby stabilize markets. In this way, assuming that euro area banks can be morally swayed to make such purchases, the ECB would indirectly provide the financing for private banks to support the euro area sovereigns. This would constitute a below-the-radar bailout of governments by the ECB through the private banking system with the political benefits to the central bank that it does not violate the EU treaty ban on monetary financing.

In summary, the December 9, 2011 EU Summit shows how the key actors in the euro area crisis are still positioning themselves to force others to pick up as much of the costs of the euro area crisis as possible. In the meantime, the crisis continues and may superficially appear to be insoluble. There are in fact several possible solutions to stave off a near term meltdown, however, when Italy and Spain begin their large bond rollovers in early 2012:

· Germany can write a check and agree to expand the EFSF/ESM and/or give it a banking license.
· The IMF can write a check using new resources from the euro area and rest of the world to put together a sizable new support program for Italy and/or Spain.
· The ECB can write a check and begin to purchase much larger amounts of the relevant sovereign bonds.

It remains to be seen which solution will ultimately be chosen. It is possible, indeed likely, that the ultimate package will combine parts of each of the above. But it is obvious that none of these solutions are even remotely as costly for any of the main actors involved, inside or outside the euro area, as a sovereign default in Italy and/or collapse of the euro. That is why, once the political pre-positioning is over and the alternatives are exhausted, the games of chicken will end and the political decision on how to split the bill for securing the euro's survival will be made.

THE REMAINING AGENDA

Even the most successful financial engineering in the euro area will ultimately fail, however, if the debtor countries, and indeed the region as a whole, are unable to restore at least modest economic growth in the fairly near future. This requires at least three major steps:

· The borrowing countries must adopt convincing pro-growth structural reforms, especially in their labor markets, as well as budgetary austerity.

· The strong economies in the northern core of Europe, especially Germany, must terminate their own fiscal consolidations for a while and adopt new expansionary measures, i.e., they should buy more Italian and Greek goods and services rather than debt instruments.

· The ECB must promptly reduce its policy interest rate by at least another 50 basis points and buy sufficient amounts of periphery bonds through the SMP to help push their interest rates down to sustainable levels.

There has been much talk about the infeasibility of achieving the needed "internal devaluations." Germany has achieved just such an adjustment over the past two decades, however, probably amounting to about 20 percent of the (overvalued) exchange rate at which it entered the ERM/euro, through a combination of budget tightening and structural changes like the Hartz labor reforms. At the other end of the size spectrum, Latvia achieved an even speedier and more spectacular correction of its huge current account deficit of 25 percent of GDP and, only three years later, is now combining renewed growth with an external surplus. Italy has previously achieved dramatic adjustment, notably to qualify for the euro in the first place. (Greece never did so and its ability to remain within the zone is clearly more problematic.)

The agenda for the euro area, and indeed Europe more broadly, thus ranges well beyond the financial engineering that is clearly the most urgent requirement to overcome the crisis. Both the history of the integration project and the revealed responses at each stage of the current turmoil, however, suggest that both the historical imperatives and economic self-interest of all the key countries, both creditor and debtor, will coalesce successfully. Watch what they do rather than what they say as the drama continues to unfold.

The final major political challenge on the euro area agenda for 2012 goes beyond measures to address the immediate crisis but rather focuses on the longer-term continuation and direction of euro area institutional reform. During 2012, the euro area is likely to adopt a new and considerably more credible set of fiscal rules and budget oversight regulation. This has been a clear demand from both the ECB and Germany. But while the new fiscal compact will undoubtedly help stabilize the euro area in the future, it must be thought of as merely a beginning of the institutional reforms needed in the region. Fiscal consolidation is not everything and the movement toward further and symmetrical deepening of euro area fiscal integration must be maintained. Following the "fiscal rules first" down payment, euro area leaders must consequently take further concrete steps in 2012 on a reasonable timetable toward the introduction of measures such as eurobonds.

It took ten years for the first serious economic and political crisis to arrive after the euro was introduced. The most challenging part of today's crisis is to use the political opportunity it presents to get the basic economic institutions right and complete the euro's half built house for the long term. In this process the euro will develop in a different manner from the full economic and monetary union established in the United States. It will require additional substantial treaty and institutional revisions in the future. But as the US Constitution's 27 current amendments clearly show, faulty initial designs need not preclude long-term success. If the history of the integration exercise and its crisis responses to date are any guide, Europe will emerge from its current turmoil not only with the euro intact but with far stronger institutions and economic prospects for the future.

The Implications for the United States and U.S. Policy

The United States has a major national interest in successful resolution of the European crisis. Europe is the largest market for US exports and by far the largest locus of US foreign investment. There are extensive financial linkages between US banks, and other financial institutions, and their European counterparts. A breakup of the Eurozone would push Europe into a sharp recession or worse with sufficient spillover to the United States to sharply truncate our (already weak) growth as well. Europe of course remains our major international ally as well and any recrudescence of intra-European conflict, which only the European integration project has been able to check, could be disastrous for US foreign policy and indeed national security.

The Europeans should of course provide the bulk of the resources needed to resolve their crisis. They are doing so already and they will do whatever else is needed.

But there may be domestic political limits on those contributions in Europe, as everywhere else, and the rest of the world may thus need to help. It did so quite usefully in the initial phase of the crisis when the International Monetary Fund provided one third of the external financing required for Greece, Ireland and Portugal. IMF involvement is highly valuable for a second reason that may be even more important than its money (although the two necessarily go hand in hand): its greater ability to devise and enforce the needed disciplines on the borrowing countries, due to its long experience with such programs and far greater ability to adopt a tough stance toward the borrowers.

There is a growing consensus that the IMF should position itself to play a similar role in Italy and Spain, the two large Eurozone borrowers, both became IMF conditionality would then be even more crucial and because their financial needs, which together could total €1 trillion, could be beyond the capability of even Germany and the other strong eurozone countries. Even if the money were never used, moreover, the creation of such a substantial "firewall" could be crucial in convincing markets that defaults by these large economies would be inconceivable and thus restoring confidence in the overall outlook.

The IMF now has about $400 billion of usable reserves. It is planning to seek loans from its member countries of $500-600 billion to create a "firewall" of the desired magnitude. The United States has a major interest in the success of this project and should support it strongly.

Many people believe that the United States, as a rich country and the traditional leader of the international monetary system, should also contribute to the exercise itself. This would be inappropriate, however. The objective is for the IMF to borrow from creditor countries that are running large trade and current account surpluses (and to channel these funds to debtor countries that are running large deficits and undertaking serious adjustment programs). The main targets should be countries with very large foreign exchange reserves: most notably China but also Japan, Russia, oil exporters in the Middle East, Korea, Brazil,

Singapore, Hong Kong and several others in Asia. Several of these countries, such as Brazil and Russia, have already indicated their readiness to contribute.

By contrast, the United States is the world's largest debtor country. We are running annual current account deficits of $500 billion or more. If we were to lend to the IMF, we would have to borrow even more from China and our own foreign creditors. It would be far better for the Fund to borrow from those countries directly.

At the same time, it is imperative that the Congress work with the Administration to pass the legislation needed to implement the IMF quota reforms agreed at the G-20 summit in Seoul in November 2011. That agreement included a doubling of the IMF's quotas, and thus its basic resources, though without any increase in total US financing for the Fund because our increased quota would be fully offset by a reduction in our commitment to one of its earlier borrowing agreements. Even more importantly, it redistributes quotas and thus voting rights at the Fund away from the grossly over-represented Europeans to the grossly under-represented emerging markets, which will be an essential part of the "grand bargain" under which they will lend substantial additional resources to the Fund to enable it help Europe on the needed scale. The US quota and voting share would change very little and we will continue to have veto power over any major IMF decisions, which is why our vote is required to implement the reform package and Congressional approval thereof is so important to promote US interests.

The United States can thus provide crucial support for resolving the European economic and financial crisis through the IMF, without spending any additional money, by supporting both the agreed quota reforms and the proposed new borrowings from major surplus countries.

The final, and very important, point is that we should understand that the euro crisis is a wakeup call for the United States as well. In the short run, the travails of the Europeans have led to large capital flows into the United States and the dollar that have contributed substantially to our very low interest rates despite our failure to seriously address our own budget problem and the related downgrade by Standard and Poor. Hence Europe has shielded us from much of the adverse effect of our own policy failures.

But we must remember that the financial markets were pricing Greek (and Irish and Portuguese and Spanish and Italian) debt at virtually the same rate as German debt only a few years ago. When reality set in, the crisis exploded very quickly and those countries were forced to adopt drastic fiscal adjustments at the worst possible time – when their own economies, and the neighborhood, were already very weak. On realistic current projections, the US deficit and debt numbers will look as bad in less than ten years than Greece's did at the onset of its national nightmare.

Hence we should regard the euro crisis as a wakeup call for ourselves rather than a source of solace that enables us to put off our day of reckoning a bit longer. The current weakness of our economy and the fact that we do have time to adjust means that we should combine short-term stimulus with decisive actions now, not just words and new procedures, that will correct our budget imbalance and debt buildup over the next three to five years. A failure to do so would mean that we have learned nothing from the euro crisis and will come to rue our failures to act as much as Greece, Italy and the other periphery debtors in Europe are now doing.

Statement Before the Hearing on
THE OUTLOOK FOR THE EUROZONE
Senate Budget Committee
United States Senate
February 1, 2012

Economic Recovery and Global Challenges

By
Robert D. Hormats
Under Secretary for Economic, Energy and Agricultural Affairs

When then-candidate Barack Obama spoke in Berlin in July 2008, he stated that one of the priorities of his presidency would be to re-establish strong trans-Atlantic relations. Citing the daunting political, security and economic challenges of the 21st century, he stressed then that —America has no better partner than Europe.‖

In the more than three years since, and despite discussion in the media about where Europe fits in the United States' global framework and speculation that Europe is turning inward as it deals with its domestic issues, the reality that President Obama articulated in Berlin has not changed. Europe is -- and remains -- America's partner of first resort and its staunchest ally. The strategic alignment between the United States and Europe, rooted in shared history and values, has never been closer in addressing both international threats and internal challenges.

America, since the days of Presidents Truman and Eisenhower, and Secretaries Marshall, Acheson and Dulles has recognized that a united and prosperous Europe is of enormous importance to the United States. And we have recognized, since the days of Jean Monnet and Robert Schuman, that closer economic integration in Europe was an essential underpinning to a stronger Europe and its ability to be a robust ally. And we understood that a prosperous Europe was important to a prosperous America. That was true in the 1950s when we supported the Marshall Plan, and it is today.

In Libya, NATO allies came together with Arab and other partners to support the Libyan people and prevent a catastrophe. In Afghanistan, with nearly 40,000 European troops on the ground alongside our own, we have built and sustained NATO's largest-ever overseas deployments. And we will continue to support the Afghans as they assume full responsibility for their own security by the end of 2014.

On Iran, along with our European allies, we share a deep and increasing concern about unresolved issues and Iran's continued refusal to comply with its international nuclear obligations. We remain committed to a dual-track policy that uses pressure to urge Iran to engage seriously on its nuclear program. 2

And the strength of this alliance with Europe depends heavily on the health of our economies. The statement of the European Council on January 30, 2012, clearly points to a renewed focus on jobs and growth, which provides new opportunities for U.S. - EU trade, investment and science and technology cooperation for our mutual benefit.

That is not to say that there are no differences across the Atlantic. But the reality is that we have essentially the same central objectives and are working on them together around the world.

Today, I'd like to comment on this reality in two areas:

First, our transatlantic work towards a common agenda of economic recovery and growth. This includes strengthening transatlantic trade and investment ties that reinforce our mutual recoveries, bringing emerging powers into the international rules-based system, and reorienting the global economic architecture for 21st century challenges; and

Second, our work together in addressing the global challenges that confront us in Afghanistan, Iran, the Middle East and North Africa, and elsewhere.

Economic Recovery Through Trade and Job Creation

Today's hearing is focused on the Eurozone crisis -- and for good reason. We have a huge stake in the health and vitality of Europe's economies. European growth is important both for the global economy and for creating and sustaining jobs in the United States.

To put this in perspective, the value of United States goods and services exports to the European Union is about five times the value of our exports to China. Trade flows between the United States and the EU exceed $2.7 billion per day.

In addition to the steps the EU has taken to resolve the debt and banking crisis, which Under Secretary Brainard has just discussed, we also have seen a commitment, as evidenced by the results of the EU Summit on January 30, to address the current economic challenges not only through fiscal consolidation, but also by facilitating job creation and putting in place measures to assist member states in finding a path back to economic growth.

There is a lot more hard work ahead. And there are many difficult choices to make. But our European partners have laid a solid foundation on which to build, and we appreciate the enormous efforts the EU has taken to regain its economic footing.

The Obama Administration is committed to expanding and deepening our economic relationship with Europe. This will help both us and our European allies sharpen our competitive edge in the global economy, and achieve our domestic objectives for economic growth and job creation. Secretary Clinton has said, "We need to forge an ambitious agenda for joint economic leadership with Europe that is every bit as compelling as our security cooperation around the world".

Transatlantic Economic Council and Regulatory Cooperation

The business community, consumer organizations and other stakeholders in the United States and in Europe have also been an active and vocal constituency in support of the Transatlantic Economic Council, or TEC. The TEC, established in 2007 and led by the White House and the European Commission, engages our most senior economic policymakers in joint work to promote economic growth and job creation on both sides of the Atlantic -- in particular by addressing regulatory barriers and fostering innovation.

As tariffs have fallen in recent decades, non-tariff measures or —behind the borderǀ barriers to trade and investment have come to pose the most significant obstacles to our trade. Regulators in both the EU and the United States aim essentially for the same strong protections for the health and safety of our citizens, for our environment, and for our financial systems.

But differing approaches to regulation and to the development of standards can create barriers and slow the growth of trade and investment. Reducing unnecessary differences can create opportunities.

One way we are seeking to minimize the impact of unnecessary regulatory divergences on trade and investment is to examine closely our respective regulatory processes, and to try to identify ways to make them more compatible and accessible. The TEC and the U.S. - EU High Level Regulatory Cooperation Forum, led by OMB, have spurred new discussion on our respective approaches to risk analysis, cost-benefit analysis, and the assessment of the impact of regulation on trade.

Among other accomplishments, one of the highlights of the November 2011 TEC meeting was arriving at a comprehensive work plan on electric vehicles and associated infrastructure, in cooperation with the U.S.-EU Energy Council, business, standard-setting bodies, and scientists on both sides of the Atlantic.

A key component of this work plan is a decision to establish —interoperability centersǀ or living laboratories, which will allow scientists from both sides of the Atlantic to share data, equipment, and testing methodologies. This in turn should set a foundation for compatible approaches and regulations in both markets and lead to interoperable e-cars and related infrastructure, such as charging stations and smart grids.

While we have a common purpose on electric vehicles, success is by no means assured. It will depend heavily on the work that is done in the private sector to prioritize and develop the standards adopted for and applied to these new technologies. The standards-setting process is very complex with vital roles for government, business and standard-setters.

If the EU and the United States can together promote the creation of compatible, high quality, transatlantic standards in a variety of sectors or product areas in the short-to- medium term, our countries can encourage other nations to adhere to them and reduce the clutter of disjointed, unilateral standards that would impede trade and serve as protectionist devices.

Businesses then will be able to deploy technologies more effectively and more quickly across the globe, where demand for these products will only grow over time, supporting our shared desire for new sources of jobs and growth.

Additionally, common transatlantic approaches to regulation can serve as a model for other nations, in particular Russia, China, Brazil and India. Together we can provide incentives for others to embrace science-based strategies and approaches, working toward regulatory convergence and enabling access to markets.

This is an important point. Many countries don't share our regulatory principles and, through regulation, try to make our companies less competitive in their markets or even try to shut them out.

The United States and the EU can both benefit if we work together to promote the adoption in third countries of market principles and internationally-accepted rules governing trade, finance, intellectual property, and investment. Better economic policies in third countries will help ensure fair competition and market access, increasing opportunities to generate exports and jobs in the United States and Europe.

U.S.-EU High Level Working Group on Jobs and Growth

At the U.S.-EU Summit in November 2011, President Obama and EU leaders pledged to make the U.S.-EU trade and investment relationship even stronger. They called upon the TEC to create a High Level Working Group on Jobs and Growth, co-chaired by the U.S. Trade Representative Ron Kirk and EU Trade Commissioner Karel De Gucht.

The purpose of this group is to identify and assess options for strengthening the transatlantic economic relationship in areas including, but not limited to: conventional barriers to trade in goods; barriers to trade in services and in investment; opportunities to reduce or prevent unnecessary non-tariff barriers to trade; and enhanced cooperation on common concerns involving third countries.

All options are on the table. USTR has had initial consultations with EU counterparts and is seeking input from all stakeholders, including Congress, as it begins its work. Several major private sector organizations have issued studies or reports that make compelling arguments for an ambitious agenda in this area.

Economic Statecraft

In October 2011, Secretary Clinton announced her vision of Economic Statecraft as a central pillar of U.S. foreign policy. An important part of that is our economic relationship with Europe. That is, how we use the tools of diplomacy abroad to support trade and the rights of U.S. investors, leverage the strengths and expertise of the U.S. private sector in our economic engagement overseas, and use diplomacy and our overseas presence to grow our economy at home by attracting foreign investment to the United States.

We have established an Economic Statecraft Task Force to elevate economic and commercial diplomacy goals and to ensure that we have the right people, support tools, and engagement platforms. The Task Force covers four principal areas of work:

human capital; internal tools; external engagement; and policy opportunities.

We are doing much of this work already, especially at our overseas posts, to support such programs as the National Export Initiative and Select USA, which promotes job-creating foreign investment in the United States. The State Department puts special emphasis on support for entrepreneurship. Under the Secretary's Economic Statecraft Initiative, we will scale up our efforts.

Some successes from recent advocacy include: Volkswagen's recent $1 billion manufacturing plant in Chattanooga, and Boeing's sale of 90 aircraft to Russian airline companies in 2011. In April 2011, helicopter producer Sikorsky won a contract worth up to $1.3 billion, to co-produce utility helicopters in Turkey.

Beyond advocacy for specific business deals, we are also working to level the playing field for U.S. workers and businesses in Europe and around the world, including in the agriculture sector. The volume of U.S. agricultural exports to the EU is strong and growing. Our 2011 agricultural exports to the EU were valued at $9.5 billion, up 8.2 % from the previous year. USDA estimates that every $1 billion in U.S. agricultural exports supports about 8,400 American jobs across a variety of sectors.

Business is telling us there is more we can do to help them grow in an increasingly challenging world. On February 21-22, Secretary Clinton is inviting 200 representatives of U.S. business support organizations and the private sector to participate in the Department's first ever Global Business Conference. This is part the Department's effort to increase engagement with the private sector and support U.S. business.

Global Challenges

We continue to work cooperatively with Europe to address the challenges that confront us both around the globe. Slower growth and tighter budgets in Europe could have an impact on some of our foreign policy objectives, but we are actively searching for more opportunities to leverage our individual and collective resources to advance our shared goals. Whatever happens on the financial and economic front, our foreign policy message has been consistent: It is important that transatlantic partners continue to dedicate resources to key priorities, and maintain critical deployments, both military and civilian. Reduced outlays overall should not mean reduced engagement in critical parts of the world.

Europe is an indispensable partner in promoting peace and prosperity through development assistance. The EU and its member states account for over 55% of global net Official Development Assistance to developing countries, with aid from the fifteen wealthiest EU member states rising by 6.7% in 2010 to just over $70 billion.

The EU and its member states have taken the lead on post-conflict aid operations in Liberia, Burundi, the Democratic Republic of the Congo, Sierra Leone, Darfur and Chad. The EU has also taken on lead roles in the democratic transitions occurring in its own neighborhood, in Libya and Tunisia and other transition countries in the Middle East and North Africa region.

Defense spending faces continued pressure in Europe. The Secretary of Defense told the Allies last fall that —we are at a critical moment for our defense partnership.Į Overall, defense spending in Europe has decreased during the past decade, but Allies are committed to keeping NATO strong through collaborative capabilities acquisitions called "Smart Defense."

Despite tight budgets, NATO allies have a strong common interest in meeting our collective security obligations and building the capabilities needed to meet 21st century security challenges. At the May 2012 NATO summit, hosted by the United States in Chicago, Allies will consider opportunities to advance our efforts on such critical capabilities as missile defense; intelligence, surveillance, and reconnaissance; and assuring the right mix of nuclear and conventional forces.

Our European allies have been critical to NATO's efforts in Afghanistan. While some feared a "rush for the exits" after NATO announced the goal of a 2014 transition to Afghan lead, in fact the Alliance has held together under the principle "in together, out together." The Chicago Summit will shape the next phase of the transition of security responsibility to the Afghan National Security Forces.

We continue to work closely with our partners in the P5+1 (the UNSC Perm 5, plus Germany) and the EU to engage Iran in serious discussions without preconditions regarding the international community's concerns about its nuclear program. As Iran has failed to show any serious sign of being ready or willing to engage, both the United States and the European Union have significantly increased our sanctions against the regime since the last round of UN sanctions in June 2010.

We believe U.S. and EU sanctions are severely affecting the regime in Iran. We see no evidence that Europe's economic crisis has made European governments less willing to impose vigorous sanctions; on the contrary, since 2011 EU member states have moved to expand dramatically measures against the regimes in Iran and Syria, including against their financial and energy sectors, and have maintained sanctions in other cases.

Most recently, on January 23, the European Union took action to ban imports of Iranian crude oil and petroleum products, freeze the assets of the Iranian central bank, and take additional action against Iran's energy, financial, and transport sectors. These actions are consistent with the Iran sanctions in the National Defense Authorization Act of 2012, on which we deeply appreciate the close engagement between the Administration and the Senate.

We will continue to coordinate with our partners in Europe and around the world to increase sanctions pressure to sharpen the choice for the Iranian regime between continued violations of its international nuclear obligations and serious engagement with negotiations. Just last month, the EU announced a dramatic extension of its sanctions regime on Iran to include a ban on imports of crude oil from Iran, the lifeblood of the Iranian economy. The EU's new sanctions mirror the new sanctions recently passed by Congress and signed into law by President Obama on December 31, 2011.

In Libya, we cooperated closely with our European allies to pass UN Security Council resolutions 1970 and 1973, which levied sanctions against the Qadhafi regime, established a no-fly zone and maritime embargo of Libya, and provided protection for citizens under attack by their own government. This authorization allowed us, in coalition with Europe, to take down Libya's air defense system. We then handed the mission over to NATO, which quickly assumed command and control, and conducted a flexible and precise operation that saved tens of thousands of lives. This operation demonstrated that NATO remains the world's strongest political-military alliance, capable of bringing Allies and partners together under one command structure in a time of crisis. Since the end of the Libya operation, the EU and our European allies have remained committed to a successful transition in Libya, through development assistance and capacity building.

The European Union and its member states have remained committed to a successful transition in Libya, through humanitarian and development assistance, as well as capacity building and technical training for the emerging Libyan government.

In Syria, the EU has joined us in steadily ratcheting up the pressure on the Asad regime, including through multiple rounds of sanctions targeting individuals responsible for abuses and institutions that fill the regime's coffers. The United States and the EU have together led efforts to call attention to Syria's human rights violations, co-sponsoring three Special Sessions in the UN Human Rights Council, one of which resulted in the creation of an independent Commission of Inquiry tasked to document the atrocities of the Asad regime. America and Europe stand united alongside the Arab League in demanding an end to the bloodshed and a democratic future for Syria.

Additionally, Germany, France and the UK (—E3|) led efforts at the UN General Assembly in November 2011 by introducing a resolution, approved by an overwhelming majority, calling on Syria to fully comply the Arab League's initiative.

And not resting on our laurels, we are engaging actively in the Middle East and North Africa to promote our shared values of democracy, especially in this time of transformational change. In the Middle East, we have a profound stake in this process. We are making the Deauville Partnership a priority during America's G-8 Presidency this year. And to make good on its promise, we will be putting forward an ambitious agenda to promote political and economic reform, trade, investment, regional integration, and entrepreneurship to help people in the region realize the better future they have risked so much to have.

And this work extends beyond the Middle East. We have to help consolidate democratic gains in places like Cote d'Ivoire and Kyrgyzstan, and support democratic openings in Burma, and wherever people lack their rights and freedom. America and Europe have more sophisticated tools than ever to support and reward those who take reforms, and to pressure those who do not.

On Russia, Europe worked with both us and the Russians last year through the long and complicated process of negotiating Russia's accession to the WTO, completing the process after 18 years of negotiation. This painstaking work resulted in an invitation to Russia to accede to this global rules-based trading system. Russia's WTO accession was a key step in putting our relations with Russia on a more constructive course, which is one of President Obama's top priorities.

Integrating Russia into the WTO has the potential to bring enormous benefits to U.S. manufacturers, farmers, and ranchers. While American exports to Russia rose 39 percent in 2011, more than twice as fast as our goods exports to the world as a whole, our exports to Russia, $8.2 billion in 2011, represents only around one-half of one percent of our total exports. 9

We should not underestimate the opportunity to expand U.S. exports further to a country of nearly 145 million people—the world's seventh largest economy. It's been estimated that Russia's WTO accession could result in a 20-percent increase in Russia's overall trade in manufactured goods, which could translate into a possible $2 billion increase in bilateral trade in manufactured goods with the United States. And the Commerce Department's International Trade Administration estimates that every billion dollars of U.S. exports supports over 5,000 jobs.

President Obama in his most recent State of the Union Address urged Congress to ensure —that no foreign company has an advantage over American manufacturing when it comes to accessing... new markets like Russia.‖ And to improve opportunities for U.S. companies in Russia going forward and support jobs here in the United States, we will need to secure the full benefits of the WTO deal for American business by terminating application of the Jackson-Vanik Amendment to

Russia, and by extending permanent normal trade relations to Russia.

Of course we have differences with Russia. Its recent veto of a tough UN resolution on Syria was – in the words of Secretary Clinton – a travesty. And the United States remains committed to strong, transparent support for civil society and democratic principles, as the Secretary demonstrated in the wake of the Russian parliamentary elections in December, when she voiced our concerns. But at the same time, we also have had unprecedented cooperation with Russia on Iran and North Korea. Russia has also agreed to greatly expanded use of its territory and airspace as supply lines to Afghanistan. And as indicated in our trade numbers, our economic ties are also expanding.

The Jackson-Vanik Amendment -- enacted vis-à-vis the former Soviet Union -- long ago fulfilled its purpose with regard to Russia: to support free emigration, particularly Jewish emigration. No such barriers to emigration exist in Russia today.

If Congress does not enact the necessary legislation to terminate Jackson-Vanik with regard to Russia, when Russia becomes a member of the WTO, the U.S. does not get all of the benefits of Russia's WTO membership, even though our competitors will. This puts many of our industries at a serious disadvantage. Unlike other WTO members, the United States will not be able to turn to the WTO mechanisms, including dispute settlement procedures, or ensure compliance on other areas such as intellectual property, services or WTO rules on antidumping.

President Obama has established extending Permanent Normal Trade Relations to Russia and terminating application of Jackson-Vanik to Russia as a major priority. Congress can help level the playing field for U.S. businesses and workers by terminating application of Jackson-Vanik to Russia before Russia joins the WTO this summer. Lifting Jackson-Vanik for Russia is about providing jobs and economic growth here in America.

Conclusion

The transatlantic relationship is not just a defining achievement of more than half a century ago – it is indispensible to the world we continue to build together in the century ahead.

Our predecessors planned for the future together. They acted on a belief that America, Europe, and like-minded nations everywhere are engaged in a single, common endeavor to build a more peaceful and prosperous and secure world. The world around us is changing fast, and America and Europe are charting our path forward together to deal with the challenges we face.

Testimony before the Senate Banking Committee
Washington, DC
February 16, 2012

European Debt Crisis Threatens the U.S. Dollar

By
Ron Paul
U.S. Representative for Texas's 14th Congressional District

The global economic situation is becoming more dire every day. Approximately half of all US banks have significant exposure to the debt crisis in Europe. Much more dangerous for the US taxpayer is the dollar's status as reserve currency for the world, and the US Federal Reserve's status as the lender of last resort. As we've learned in recent disclosures, this has not only benefitted companies like AIG, the auto industry and various US banks, but multiple foreign central banks as they have run into trouble. Nothing has been solved, however, by offering up the productivity of Americans as a sacrificial lamb. Greece is set to be the first domino to fall in the string of European economies at risk. Rather than learning from Greece's terrible example of an over-consuming public sector and drowning private sector, what is more likely from our politicians is an eventual bailout of European investors.

The US has a relatively small exposure to overwhelmed Greek banks, but much larger economies in Europe are set to follow and that will have serious implications for US banks. Greece is technically small enough to bail out. Italy is not. Germany is not. France is not. It is estimated that US banks have over a trillion dollars tied up in at-risk German and French banks. Because the urge to paper over the debt with more credit is so strong, the collapse of the Euro is imminent. Will the Fed be held responsible if the Euro brings the US dollar down with it?

The most disingenuous aspect of the narrative about the European sovereign debt crisis is that entire economies will collapse if more resources are not bilked from productive people around the world. This is untrue. Tough times are coming for the banks, to be sure, but free people always find a way back to prosperity if the politicians leave them alone. Communities within Greece are coming together and forming barter systems because they know the Euro is becoming unstable. Greeks are learning how to engage in commerce with each other, without the use of fiat currency controlled by central banks. In other words, they are rediscovering what money really is, and they are trading with each other in ways that cannot be controlled, manipulated, squandered, inflated away and generally ruined by corrupt bankers and the politicians that enable them. Farmers will still grow food, mechanics will still fix cars, people will still make things and exchange them with each other. No banker, no politician can stop that by destroying one medium of exchange. People will find or create another medium of exchange.

Unfortunately when politicians try to monopolize currency with legal tender laws, the people find it harder and harder to survive the inflation and taxation to which they are subjected. Bankers should take their dreaded haircut rather than making innocent people pay for their mistakes. The losses should be limited and liquidated, rather than perpetuated and rewarded. This is the only way we can recover.

Government debt is often considered rock solid because it is backed by a government's ability to forcibly extract interest payments out of the public. The public is increasingly unwilling to be bilked to make bankers whole. The riots and the violence in Greece should tell us something about the sustainability of this system.

If we continue to bail out banks and bankers so they can continue to lose money, if we cavalierly put this burden on the taxpayer, it is all too predictable what will happen here.

The Transatlantic Alliance

By
Jacob Funk Kirkegaard
Peterson Institute for International Economics

The European debt crisis is characterized by an extreme degree of complexity, as the correct diagnosis is not one, but at least four deep, overlapping and mutually reinforcing crises – a crisis of institutional design, a fiscal crisis, a crisis of competitiveness, and a banking crisis.

None of the four crises can be solved in isolation and no single comprehensive solution to end the crisis promptly is available to EU policymakers, meaning the drawn-out inconclusive crisis containment efforts witnessed in Europe since early 2010 will continue.

At their summit last week, euro area leaders agreed on a new set of measures, which while inadequate in scope to end the crisis and calm financial market volatility will help militate against a new dramatic economic deterioration in Europe. The risk of catastrophic spillovers from Europe to the U.S. and global economy has therefore been reduced.

The euro area has agreed a voluntary bond swap agreement with private holders of Greek government debt resulting in a 50 percent reduction in the nominal debt value. This is an urgently needed measure, which however will not independently restore Greek fiscal solvency. Meanwhile, as concerns over fiscal sustainability in the euro area stretches also to Italy, a country "too big to bailout", the principal challenge is how to avoid contagion and how to ringfence Greece so as to avoid a generalized undermining of the "risk free status" of euro area government debt.

To achieve this goal, substantial financial support will in the years ahead have to be made available to Greece, as well as Ireland and Portugal. Such resources should overwhelmingly come from the euro area, with a component provided by the IMF. Ultimately though euro area fiscal stability will only be achieved through the longer-term domestic consolidation and reform efforts particularly in Italy.

The Greek debt swap is a voluntary transaction which looks unlikely to trigger sovereign default swaps. Apart from the superficial political pride available to European leaders from being able rhetorically to deny that a euro area default has taken place, a potential short-term source of dislocation in the financial markets has hereby been removed, as – although the net outstanding Greek CDS contract value amount to less than $4bn – little is known about the extent of individual, including U.S. financial institutions' gross CDS exposures.

However, the lack of payout after a 50 percent reduction in debt may ultimately lead to the demise of the sovereign CDS product class for at least industrialized nations. Financial markets will be certain to in the future doubt whether any advanced economy sovereign debt restructuring will trigger CDS protection. Given the multiple hedging purposes for sovereign CDS, this may ironically lead in increased financial market volatility in the future, including here in the United States.

Euro area leaders secondly agreed to raise the capital requirements in banks to 9 percent core tier 1 equity and adjust for the effects of market prices of sovereign debt. This is a helpful further step, which will help insulate also U.S. financial institutions against the risk of sudden bank collapses in Europe, but will not make Europe's banking system "stable and well capitalized". Substantially more new capital and an end to the solvency concerns surrounding several euro area sovereigns themselves will be required to restore market confidence in the stability of the European banking system.

Thirdly, euro area leaders agreed on two options to boost the financial firepower of the European Financial Stability Facility (EFSF). Both are, however, are almost certain to fail. Option one, *"to provide credit enhancement to new debt issued by Member States1"* is meaningless from a systemic euro area stability point of view. When the overlap between the insurer and the insured is as big as in the euro area, the beneficial financial effects will be minimal.

Option two foresees the creation of special purpose investment vehicles open to investments from *"private and public financial institutions and investors"*. However, few if any such investors exist with the willingness and ability to invest the hundreds of billions of euros required to make a material difference for European financial stability. China will not bail Europe out and certainly, it would not be prudent use of U.S. taxpayers' money to contribute, just as the statutes of the IMF in all probability will prevent it from participating.

Fortunately though this does not matter, as the EFSF's principal purpose is political not financial. The two EFSF options described are a smokescreen created to provide political cover for the European Central Bank (ECB) to remain directly involved in the European crisis stabilization measures. This is critical, as only the ECB commands the resources to stabilize Europe.

Europe is America's largest trade and investment partner and extensive cross-ownership of large financial institutions exist. It is consequently inescapable that the U.S. domestic economy will experience a further negative external shock from any rapid deterioration of the European debt crisis.

However, the possible direct actions by U.S. policymakers have been limited by the fact that it is, despite increasing global spillover potential, still at heart a domestic economic crisis inside another sovereign jurisdiction. The ability of the U.S. government to bilaterally affect the outcome of the European debt crisis is consequently and appropriately limited. Yet, the U.S. government representatives have since the beginning of the euro area crisis exercised important indirect pressure through multilateral channels and especially the IMF and the G-20 to expedite the European crisis resolution process and push it in generally beneficial directions. The debt crisis will lead to substantial changes in European political, economic and defense potential. The crisis will with certainty lead to a more institutionally integrated euro area, potentially enabling the more coordinated projection of the continent's remaining capabilities, potentially creating an enhanced European partnership role for the U.S. The fact that the United Kingdom is unlikely to be part of a deeper integration of the euro area will however especially from the perspective of the United States be a complicating factor. The multifaceted character of the European crisis ensures that it will only be solved through a lengthy and volatile process. Yet ultimately Europe's crisis can and will be solved through the use of overwhelmingly European financial resources.

The Origin, Overlaps, and Mutual Reinforcement of the Euro's Four Crises

The euro area crisis has gradually since May 2010 taken center-place in an increasingly volatile global economy. It has become evident that the crisis consists of four distinct, though frequently overlapping and mutually reinforcing crises; 1) A design crisis, as the euro area from its creation in the 1990s has lacked crucial institutions to ensure financial stability during a crisis; 2) A fiscal crisis centered in Greece, but present across the southern euro area and Ireland; 3) A competitiveness crisis manifest in large and persistent pre-crisis current account deficits in the euro area periphery and even larger intra-euro area current account imbalances; and 4) A banking crisis first visible in Ireland, but spreading throughout euro area via accelerating concerns over sovereign solvencies.

The Euro Area Design Challenge

The concrete thinking about an economic and monetary union (EMU) in Europe goes back to 1970, when the *Werner Report*2 laid out a detailed three stage plan for the establishment of EMU in Europe by 1980. Members of the European Community would gradually increase coordination of economic and fiscal policies, while reducing exchange rate fluctuations and finally fixing these irrevocably. The collapse of the Bretton Woods system and the first oil crisis in the early 1970s caused the Werner Report proposals to be abandoned.

By the mid-1980s, following the 1979 creation of the European Monetary System and the initiation of Europe's internal market, European policymakers again took up the idea of EMU. The *Delors Report*3 from 1989 envisioned the achievement of EMU by 1999, moving gradually (again in three stages) towards closer economic coordination among the EU members, with binding constraints on member states' national budgets, and a single currency with an independent European Central Bank (ECB).

While Europe's currency union therefore has lengthy historical roots, it was an unforeseen shock – German reunification in October 1990 – that provided the political impetus for the creation of the Maastricht Treaty4, which in 1992 provided the legal foundation and detailed design for today's euro area. With the historical parity in Europe between (West) Germany and France no longer a political and economic reality, French president Francois Mitterrand and German Chancellor Helmut Kohl launched the EMU process as a principally political project to irrevocably join the French, German and other European economies together in an economic and monetary union and cement European unity.

This political imperative for launching the euro by 1999, however, frequently facilitated that politically necessary compromises, rather than theoretically sound and rigorous rules and regulations made up the institutional framework for the euro.

While the earlier Werner and Delors reports discussing the design of EMU had been explicit about the requirement to compliment a European monetary union (e.g. the common currency) with a European economic union complete with binding constraints on member states' behavior, political realities in Europe made this goal unattainable within the timeframe dictated by political leaders following German reunification.

The continued principal self-identification among Europeans as first and foremost residents of their home country5, i.e. Belgians, Germans, Poles, Italians etc., made the collection of direct taxes to fund a large centralized European budget implausible. The frequently discussed relatively high willingness of Europeans to pay taxes does not "extend to Brussels". The designers of the euro area was consequently compelled to create the common currency area without a sizable central fiscal authority with the ability to counter regional specific (asymmetric) economic shocks or re-instill confidence in private market participants in the midst of a crisis – like the one the euro area is currently experiencing.

Similarly, the divergence in the economic starting points among the politically prerequisite "founding members" of the euro area moreover made the imposition of firm, objective fiscal criteria for membership in the euro area politically impossible. The Maastricht Treaty in principle included at least two hard "convergence criteria" for euro area membership – the so-called "reference values" of 3 percent general government annual deficit limit and 60 percent general government gross debt limit6. However, in reality these threshold values were anything but fixed, as the Maastricht Treaty Article 104c stated that countries could exceed the 3 percent deficit target, if "*the ratio has declined substantially and continuously and reached a level that comes close to the reference value*", or "*excess over the reference value is only exceptional and temporary and the ratio remains close to the reference value*". Euro area countries could similarly exceed the 60 percent gross debt target, provided that "*the ratio is sufficiently diminishing and approaching the reference value at a satisfactory pace*".

In other words, it was a wholly political decision whether a country could become a member of the euro area or not, and had relatively less to do with the fundamental economic strengths and weaknesses of the country in question. As it was politically inconceivable to launch the euro without Italy, the third largest economy in continental Europe, or Belgium, home of the European capital Brussels, both countries became members despite in 1997-98 having gross debt levels of almost twice the reference value of 60 percent.

As a result, Europe's monetary union was launched in 1999 comprising of a set of countries that were far more diverse in their economic fundamentals and far less economically integrated than had been envisioned in the earlier Werner and Delors reports. Yet, not only did European political leaders proceed with the launch of the euro with far more dissimilar countries than what economic theory would have predicted feasible, shortly after the launch of the euro, they went further and undermined the remaining credibility of the rules-based framework for the coordination of national fiscal policies in the euro area.

Building on the euro area convergence criteria, the Stability and Growth Pact (SGP) was intended to safeguard sound public finances, prevent individual euro area members from running unsustainable fiscal policies and thus guard against moral hazard by enforcing budget discipline. However, faced themselves with breaching the 3 percent deficit limit in 2002-2004, France and Germany pushed through a watering down of the SGP rules in March 20057 that, as in the Maastricht Treaty itself, introduced sufficient flexibility into the interpretation of SGP that its enforcement became wholly political and with only limited reference to objective economic facts. Individual euro members subsequently failed to restore the long-term sustainability of their finances during the growth years before the global financial crisis began.

By 2005 the euro area was as a result of numerous shortcuts taken to achieve and sustain a political goal, a common currency area consisting of a very dissimilar set of countries, without a central fiscal agent, without any credible enforcement of budget discipline or real deepening economic convergence.

Initially, however, none of these danger signs mattered, as the financing costs in private financial markets of all euro area members quickly fell towards the traditionally low interest rates of Germany.

It is beyond this testimony to speculate about the causes of this lasting colossal mispricing of credit risk in the euro area.. The financial effects of this failure on the other hand were obvious, as euro area governments and private investors were able to finance themselves at historically low (often significantly negative real) interest rates seemingly irrespective of their economic fundamentals. Large public and private debt overhangs were correspondingly built up in the euro area during the first years of the euro area and in the run up to the global financial crisis in 2008. Financial markets' failure to properly assess the riskiness of different euro area countries papered over these issues until the global financial crisis finally struck.

The euro area institutional design has in essence been that of a "fair weather currency", with no central institutions capable of compelling the member states to act in unison. As a new, untested and severely under-institutionalized entity, the euro area has had no capacity to act forcefully during the current crisis or restore confidence among private businesses and consumers. Unless that changes, the euro area will be unable to exit the current crisis.

European policymakers therefore today are faced with the acute challenge of correcting the design flaws in the euro area institutions that their predecessors in their quest to quickly realize a political vision for Europe helped create. The euro area needs a new rule book. Leaders must in the midst of this crisis craft a new set of euro area institutions that for the first time provide the common currency with binding fiscal rules for its member states, and a centralized fiscal entity capable of acting in a crisis on behalf of the euro area as a whole. This will require the transfer of sovereignty from individual member states to the supra-national euro area level considerably beyond what has previously occurred in the EU.

The Euro Area Fiscal Challenge

The euro area fiscal crisis is concentrated in Greece, which according to the latest IMF/EC/ECB estimates will have a general government debt surpassing 180 percent of GDP by 2012. Despite Greece's IMF program and associated financial support from the EU and IMF since May 2010, the country is at this point clearly not able to repay all its creditors in full and has to restructure its government debt. Greece will consequently be the first ever euro area country and first OECD member since shortly after World War 2 forced to restructure its sovereign debt.

Portugal and Ireland are currently subject to IMF programs, too, but in contrast to Greece have successfully implemented their program commitments to this date8. Through continued strong reform implementation and access to financial assistance from the EU and IMF in the years ahead, it looks still potentially feasible for Portugal and Ireland to in the medium-term restore their access to private financial markets at sustainable interest rates.

However, the cost of financing for Spain and Italy has also risen substantially in recent month with secondary 10y bond market yields currently between 5.5 and 6 percent. Unlike, however, the three smaller euro area countries with IMF programs, Spain and Italy are economies of a size that makes them "too big to bailout" for the euro area, even with IMF help. The fact that financial markets have begun to doubt the fiscal sustainability of "too big to bailout" members of the euro area is at the heart of the euro area policy makers' fiscal challenge.

The key link between Greece and Spain and Italy is the issue of "contagion"9, i.e. a situation in which instability in a specific asset markets or institutions is transmitted to one or more other specific such asset markets or institutions. Inside a currency union like the euro area, where the central bank is legally barred from guaranteeing all the sovereign debts of individual member states10 and the for political reasons each sovereign members' debts remains distinct11, yet the debt is denominated in the same currency and governed by at least some common institutions, the phenomenon of contagion has particular force. If private investors begin to fear that a precedent will be set inside the euro area with the imposition of haircuts on Greek sovereign debt, they will assess the riskiness of other euro area members' sovereign debt differently once the "risk free status" of euro area sovereign debt has been impaired. The large increases in the interest rates on Italian and Spanish government debt seen immediately following the July 21st, 2011 EU Council decision to first introduce haircuts on Greek government debt looks, in the absence of simultaneous new bad economic news released from the two countries, to be largely due to contagion.

Given the high public and private debt levels built up before the global financial crisis in Spain and Italy, the sudden emergence of contagion and associated reprising by private investors of the riskiness of these two countries has the potential initiate destabilizing self-fulfilling interest rate-solvency spirals. Contagion from Greece causes Italian interest rates to go up, which given Italy's high existing debt levels adds materially to the interest burden, necessitating further austerity measures, further reducing economic growth in the short-term, leading to lower government revenues and increased financial market concerns, again increasing both the Italian government deficit and interest burden. The presence of contagion inside a currency union, where many individual members have high debt levels consequently have to potential of turning what might previously have been stable and sustainable high debt burdens into unstable unsustainable debt burdens.

The unique degree of independence of the ECB adds a further complication to such contagion inside the euro area. Its independence derives from Article 282 of the EU Treaty12, which states that the central bank "*shall be independent in the exercise of its powers and in the management of its finances. Union institutions, bodies, offices and agencies, and the governments of the Member States shall respect that independence.*" With Treaty-defined independence, the ECB is more akin to a Supreme Court than a central bank in the mold of the U.S. Federal Reserve, whose independence is derived from the Federal Reserve Act passed by Congress (which Congress expressly reserves the right to amend, alter, or repeal13). The ECB has no political masters and the EU Treaty moreover bars bar elected officials from criticizing its decisions.

In a sovereign and financial crisis, such total central bank independence might actually hinder the restoration of market confidence, because it might further undermine investors' trust in the solvency of a government that does not ultimately control its own central bank, lacks its own currency, and thus has no ultimate lender of last resort. The European Treaty's Article 123 forbids the ECB to extend credit to member states, preventing it from issuing any blanket guarantees for their sovereign debt. Due to the complete independence of the ECB and the restrictions the EU Treaty places on it, the euro area thus lacks an important confidence boosting measure in the face of contagion.

On the other hand, the ECB's independence and status as the only pan-euro area institution capable of direct forceful action to calm global financial markets bestows upon the ECB's governing council a degree of leverage over elected officials in this crisis not seen elsewhere in the world. This gives the ECB leadership the ability to engage in horse-trading with democratically elected governments behind closed doors, where it can quietly demand that government leaders implement far-reaching reforms. A clear example of this came in August 2011 just ahead of the ECB's initiation of emergency support purchases of Italian government debt. The sitting and incoming presidents of the ECB wrote bluntly to Italian Prime Minister Silvio Berlusconi , stating that "the [ECB] Governing Council considers that pressing action by the Italian authorities is essential to restore the confidence of investors14" followed by a list of more than ten specific required reforms to be implemented by the Italian government.

The degree of independence and influence of the ECB matters for the attempts to find an expeditions solution to the euro area fiscal crisis, as it is actually not in the ECB's interest to act too decisively to immediately try to end any contagion or the crisis more broadly. It is not that the ECB cannot step in. There is no asset it cannot buy, if the governing council agrees. The strategy of allowing financial market mayhem to pressure European governments is therefore less risky than it seems. Ultimately, the ECB has the means to calm markets down but its intention is to do so only to avoid absolute disaster.

A sweeping preemptive "helping hand to euro area governments" under speculative attack would from the perspective of the ECB be counterproductive, as it would relieve pressure on governments to reform. The ECB's game is thus not to end the crisis at all costs as soon as possible, but to act deliberatively to cajole governments into implementing the crisis solutions it wants. The market volatility seen accelerating in recent months becomes something not to be avoided, but to use as a club against recalcitrant and reform-resistant euro area leaders.

European policymakers therefore today are faced with the acute challenge of enabling Greece to restructure its unsustainable sovereign debt, while at the same time ensuring that such an event has no precedent-setting effects inside the euro area and that contagion among sovereign debt markets consequently is contained. Ring-fencing Greece geographically and in the time dimension (i.e. assuring that Greece will only ever go through a single one-off sovereign debt restructuring) will require further financial assistance in the coming years be provided to Greece itself, as well as Portugal and Ireland. The sizable majority of this support must sensible come from the rest of the euro area, with some continued financial participation also of the IMF.

In addition to further restrict contagion, euro area leaders must device a method which can provide a degree of preemptive financial support to "too big to bailout" euro area members and potentially lower their primary bond market cost of finance. This is the key aspect of the current debate surrounding how to utilize the €440bn European Financial Stability Facility (EFSF) most effectively. However, given the constraints on and reluctance of the ECB to participate directly in any such financial support (though for instance providing leverage to the EFSF) to large non-IMF program countries, the resources available to euro area leaders will be constrained. Any financial benefits to large beneficiary countries like Spain and Italy from new euro area measures will moreover be relatively limited, due to the large weight inside the euro area itself of the beneficiary countries themselves. Irrespective of the ultimate format chosen by euro area leaders, the "correlation between benefactors and beneficiaries" will be so large that the financial advantage will be relatively modest. There will be no euro area "bazooka" created from the EFSF. Ultimately, the euro area will have to rely on its large members to "bail themselves out" through a lengthy period of fiscal consolidation. Financial markets are unlikely to be satisfied with this outcome, and while the ECB will continue to act as a conditional final defender of financial stability in the euro area, heightened levels of uncertainty and volatility will remain a feature of the euro area sovereign debt and other asset markets several years ahead.

The Euro Area Competitiveness Challenge

The euro area was wrought by merging together in a single currency a number of highly divergent European economies, and for reasons of political expediency any binding political euro area rules and intrusive regulations that could during the euro's first decade have forced a real economic convergence to occur among divergent euro area members were abandoned. Cushioned by the seemingly secure access to cheap financing once inside the euro area, most member states moreover scaled back the implementation of structural reforms of their national economies15.

The principal exception was Germany, which in the years immediately after the euro introduction implemented a series of far reaching reforms of especially its labor markets and pension system. Consequently, Europe's traditionally strongest and most competitive economy during the first decade of the euro area gradually pulled itself even further ahead of most of the other members of the common currency. A persistent pattern inside the euro area consequently became the widening current account imbalances with Germany and other Northern members running surpluses and especially the Southern peripheral members running deficits.

Financing their large external deficits posed few obstacles for peripheral countries prior to the global financial crisis, even as it became clearer that the inflows of foreign capital were increasingly channeled towards financing speculative real estate investments, rather than adding to new productive asset investments. With the disappearance of foreign private capital following the onslaught of the global financial crisis, peripheral euro area deficit countries and their banks suddenly found themselves instead overwhelmingly dependent on financial support from the ECB. However, while such central support will be continuous inside any functioning currency union, a longer-term requirement for peripheral euro area nations to regain competitiveness and restore external balance (or surplus) remains16. Without improving external competitiveness and increasing exports/reducing imports, the euro area periphery will not during their current prolonged period of fiscal consolidation be able to restore domestic economic growth.

Inside a currency union without the ability to devalue their currency against major trading partners, peripheral euro area members, however, do not have access to the traditionally fastest and most effective way through which a country can regain external competitiveness17. Consequently, the euro area peripheral countries only have means at their disposal to increase the competitiveness that might be effective in a longer-term framework. Such measures include numerous traditional "supply-side structural reforms" of especially peripheral euro area labor markets, where the often legally sanctioned coercive power of labor unions, the rigidity of collective bargaining agreements and automatic wage indexation to the public sector must be curtailed. Nominal wage levels at the firm level must be brought into line with productivity, an effort which in numerous instances will lead to nominal wage cuts.

European policymakers face a competitiveness challenge today in which the precise requirements of the euro area periphery to regain their external competitiveness and for the euro area as a whole to limit intra-euro area imbalances will vary depending on individual country circumstances and require additional measures in surplus countries (such as Germany), too. It is furthermore evident that available policy options inside a currency union are of a structural reform character. Such reforms can only hope to be effective in raising competitiveness and potential economic growth rates in the medium term, and will indeed in the short term, though for instance required nominal wage declines, hurt economic growth.

The Euro Area Banking Crisis

The first manifestations of a banking crisis in the euro area in Ireland in 2008 had relatively few pan-euro area elements about it. The Irish real estate boom was clearly supported by the record low negative real interest rates in the country following the introduction of the euro, but the 2008 collapse of the Irish banking sector and subsequent required rescue of the Irish government by the EU and IMF was overwhelmingly due to domestic Irish domestic factors and failures18. That on the other hand is not true of the most recent volatility to affect the euro area banking system.

Several systematic ailments plague the euro area banking system; First of all, the euro area's banking system is very large relative to the size of the overall home economies with average euro area financial institutions' gross debt equal to 143 percent of GDP (U.S. equal 94 percent). Secondly, euro area bank leverage is very high at tangible assets at 26 times common equity (U.S. level is at 12 times); and thirdly, euro area banks tend to own a lot of the debt issued by their own governments (something U.S. banks do to a much smaller degree).

The sheer size of the euro area banking system makes it – as illustrated in Ireland in 2008-10 – problematic for individual already indebted euro area governments to credibly issue guarantees to stand behind their domestic banks in a crisis. This issue is aggravated by the low level of common equity (core tier 1) capital in the euro area banks. With low private shareholder risk capital levels in euro area banks, euro area governments risks being frequently called upon to rescue domestic banks as only a thin layer of private equity capital is available as first-loss risk capital. Disproportionally large capital injection requirements are another risk to euro area tax payers in rescues of thinly capitalized banks. There is consequently across the euro area a large degree of interdependence between the financial solidity of large domestic banking systems and national government solvency.

The bank large ownership of government debt in the euro area presents a particularly intractable concern. Euro area (and other) banks are under the Basle Agreements not required to set aside any risk capital to offset any future losses on government bond holdings. Sovereign bonds have by definition been deemed "risk free". Consequently, when Greek government debt must be restructured, it will impose upon the euro area banks credit losses for which they have previously not set aside capital, and given the scale of ownership of such debt among domestic Greek banks will require that these be recapitalized with money from international donors. The same dynamic is inevitable across essentially all euro area members, as the domestic banking system will face ruinous capital losses if national sovereign debt is restructured, due to the high domestic government debt ownership.

Fearful that banks would require very large amounts of new equity capital, which would in many instances have to come from governments themselves and might therefore pose a challenge to some governments' own solvency, European banking regulators have been reluctant to include any potential impairment of banks' sovereign debt holdings in EU bank stress tests in 2010 and 2011. Given, however, the justified market concerns about the solvency of at least one euro area sovereign (Greece) and the potential for contagion to other euro area sovereign bond markets, stress tests that do not include the potential for losses on sovereign bonds cannot provide a credible measure of the riskiness of any euro area banking system. As long as solvency concerns exists about euro area governments, a high degree of volatility will surround the euro area banking system, which again provide a powerful feedback loop to increased investor fears about the financial stability of governments in the first place.

Lastly, in addition to low capital levels and associated concerns, many euro area banks also suffer from substantial liquidity risks with high degrees of dependence on short-term wholesale funding from markets where access may prove ephemeral and subject to rapid changes.

Euro area governments face the challenge of rapidly having to stabilize their oversized and in the aggregate undercapitalized banking systems without having to dispend large amounts of capital themselves, as this could further jeopardize their own solvency. Further postponement today of forceful measures to stabilize the euro area banking system with new outside capital risks throwing the euro area into an accelerating credit crunch as banks de-lever and conserve their scarce capital. This would rapidly have a strongly detrimental effect on the broader growth prospects of the euro area.

Not all euro area governments are in the same situation though, as for instance the German government would quite easily be able to manage an even very large government-led recapitalization of its national banking system. However, due to the close linkages among sovereigns (and consequently their banking systems) inside the euro area and the observable presence of contagion between them, a key challenge for European policymakers will be to move expeditiously to a new system of tougher pan- European banking support, regulation and supervision. The establishment of a new set of common regulatory institutions for the European banking system will, however, due to the obvious implications potential government financial crisis support for banks have for governments' own solvency require a new level of fiscal integration in the euro area and the commensurate loss of national fiscal sovereignty.

The fact that the City of London, the EU and euro area financial center, is located in the UK, which can safely be assumed to remain outside the euro area itself for the foreseeable future, further complicates this type of banking sector integration initiatives.

The European Debt Crisis

1 See Euro Area Summit Statement at
http://www.consilium.europa.eu/uedocs/cms_data/docs/pressdata/en/ec/125
644.pdf.

2 Available at http://aei.pitt.edu/1002/1/monetary_werner_final.pdf.

3 Available at http://aei.pitt.edu/1007/1/monetary_delors.pdf.

4 Available at http://www.eurotreaties.com/maastrichtec.pdf.

5 See Kirkegaard (2010) at http://www.piie.com/publications/pb/pb10-25.pdf.

6 The actual numerical reference values to article 104c of the Maastricht Treaty are in a Protocol on the Excessive Deficit Procedure to the Treaty. Available at http://www.eurotreaties.com/maastrichtprotocols.pdf. The Maastricht Convergence Criteria for euro area membership eligibility include three additional metrics; inflation (within 1.5 percent of the three EU countries with the lowest inflation rate); long-term interest rates (within 2 percent of the three lowest interest rates in the EU); and exchange rate fluctuations (participation for two years in the ERM II narrow band of exchange rate fluctuations).

7 See EU Council Conclusions March 23rd 2005 at
http://www.consilium.europa.eu/uedocs/cms_data/docs/pressdata/en/ec/843
35.pdf.

8 See IMF press release 11/374 at
 http://www.imf.org/external/np/sec/pr/2011/pr11374.htm and IMF press release 11/330 at http://www.imf.org/external/np/sec/pr/2011/pr11330.htm.

9 See speech by ECB vice-president Vitor Constancio for a precise definition and discussion at
http://www.ecb.int/press/key/date/2011/html/sp111010.en.html.

10 Article 123 in the EU Treaty states "*Overdraft facilities or any other type of credit facility with the European Central Bank or with the central banks of the Member States (hereinafter referred to as 'national central banks') in favour of Union institutions, bodies, offices or agencies, central governments, regional, local or other public authorities, other bodies governed by public law, or public undertakings of Member States shall be prohibited, as shall the purchase directly from them by the European Central Bank or national central banks of debt instruments.*"

11 As discussed above, with the vast majority of European citizens still self-identifying as citizens of their respective countries (rather than the euro area), a pooling of all the national sovereign debts of the euro area into a single debt instruments - similar to what Alexander Hamilton achieved for the U.S. states' war debts in 1790 - is not a realistic political option in Europe at this point. Another critical political difference is that unlike the war debts incurred by U.S. states during the Revolutionary War, the outstanding debts of individual euro area members have not been incurred in order to achieve a "common cause". The political narrative of seeing such debts "honored in common" by all euro area members consequently does not exist.

12 http://www.ecb.int/ecb/legal/pdf/fxac08115enc_002.pdf.

13 http://www.federalreserve.gov/aboutthefed/section31.htm

14 Full text of ECB letter to Silvio Berlusconi at
http://www.corriere.it/economia/11_settembre_29/trichet_draghi_inglese_304
a5f1e-ea59-11e0-ae06- 4da866778017.shtml?fr=correlati.

91

15 See Duval and Elmeskov (2005) for an in-depth analysis at http://www.ecb.int/pub/pdf/scpwps/ecbwp596.pdf.

16 It can be seen how peripheral deficits have declined substantially since 2008. This, however, can be mostly related to the severe economic contractions experienced in the euro area periphery, which has temporarily caused import levels to collapse.

17 I shall in this testimony not discuss the option of member leaving the euro area. I will refrain from this for three main reasons; first of all, I consider the costs of any country leaving the euro area as catastrophically high for the country in question, irrespective of whether it is Greece or Germany. Secondly, it is clear from the political announcements of all EU leaders that the departure of any country from the euro area will not be tolerated (such a departure could prove to have a very serious contagion effect). And thirdly, as under the current EU Treaty, the departure from the euro area is legally undefined and thus presumed impossible.

18 See the Nyberg Report at

http://www.bankinginquiry.gov.ie/Documents/Misjuding%20Risk%20-%20Causes%20of%20the%20Systemic%20Banking%20Crisis%20in%20Ireland.pdf.

Testimony before the U.S. Senate Foreign Relations Subcommittee on European Affairs,
November 2nd, 2011

Foreign Policy and Security Policy

By
Bruce Stokes
Senior Transatlantic Fellow for Economics
German Marshall Fund of the United States

America has a huge economic stake in Europe finally resolving its crisis. A European "Lost Decade" would do profound damage to the U.S. economy.

But the euro crisis is no longer simply an economic problem. It is increasingly a foreign and security policy challenge for the United States.

And this crisis has the potential to undermine the transatlantic alliance, something the Soviets never accomplished during the Cold War.

Default by one or more euro area countries could well lead to stagnant economic growth, introspection and self-preoccupation in Europe. A weakened, distracted Europe would prove a strategic liability for the United States.

It would mean a Europe even less able to defend itself. One that cuts back on foreign aid. A Europe that falls short in its effort to curb greenhouse gases. That becomes dependent on China to fund its debt. That is less able to stand up to Russian energy blackmail. Or to impose trade sanctions to curb Iran's nuclear ambitions.

A Europe where the standard of living is declining could also face a growing public backlash in the form of rising nationalism and populism that could pull Europe apart. And a disintegrating Europe would only accelerate America's drift toward an Asian-centric foreign policy. A development that is neither in Europe's, nor America's self-interest.

A Europe that is tearing itself apart will be, by definition, less strong. And a Europe that is less strong will be less useful for the United States.

In this regard, the most immediate strategic problem for the United States created by the euro crisis will be the coming, inevitable budget austerity in Europe. Belt tightening is already eroding European capacity to share the burden of paying for global public goods.

European defense spending has dropped almost two percent annually for a decade and more cuts are in the works. The cost of short changing defense was evident in the Libyan conflict, where Britain and France would not have been able to carry out their successful mission without U.S. munitions. Faced with our own budgetary constraints, longstanding American resentment about Europe's lack of burden sharing is only likely to grow, poisoning future defense collaboration.

More broadly, the euro crisis is undermining Europe's pivotal job as a democratic, free-market role model for its immediate neighbors. The nations of Central and Eastern Europe joined the European Union to share in its affluence and political stability. Now the EU looks to be a club of austerity, pain and political impotence.

In the future, association with the European economy may no longer look so attractive to Turkey, accelerating its trajectory as an unpredictable and unhelpful free agent in the Middle East. Similarly, as the EU looks less stable and successful, the former nations of the Soviet Union are likely to slip further back into Moscow's orbit.

With the stability of North Africa in doubt and the Balkans still unsettled, the last thing Washington needs is for the European Union to become a centrifugal force in the region.

Finally, European preoccupation with the euro crisis could dash all American hope for transatlantic cooperation in coping with China. Beijing is flexing its muscles in the South China Sea and the Indian Ocean. It is extending its influence in Pakistan, in Africa and Latin America. It is developing its own brand of Chinese state capitalism that certainly looks more attractive to many around the world than that being practiced in Europe or, I dare say, even in the United States. Washington will be hard pressed to counter this Chinese influence on its own. And we could find ourselves without an effective European partner.

The euro crisis is a crisis of Europe's military and diplomatic leadership and vision. And, as Europe's strategic partner for the last two generations, Europe's problems are now our headache. It is imperative that the United States do whatever it can to help Europe resolve its current economic troubles.

Testimony before the U.S. Senate Committee on Foreign Relations
Subcommittee on European Affairs
"The European Debt Crisis: Strategic Implications for the
Transatlantic Alliance"
November 2, 2011

The Eurozone Debt Crisis and the United States

By

Desmond Lachman

Resident Fellow American Enterprise Institute

The views expressed in this testimony are those of the author alone and do not necessarily represent those of the American Enterprise Institute.

There will be a further significant intensification of the Euro-zone debt crisis in the months immediately ahead. The efforts currently underway by European policymakers to address this crisis will fall short of what might be needed to resolve this crisis in an orderly fashion. There are serious risks that the Eurozone crisis poses to the US economic recovery.

Origins of the Crisis

1. The main underlying cause of the Eurozone debt crisis is that countries in the **Eurozone's periphery persistently did not play by the currency union's rules**. In particular, whereas the Maastricht Treaty had proscribed member countries from running budget deficits in excess of 3 percent of GDP, Greece, Ireland, and Portugal all ran budget deficits well above 10 percent of GDP. Similarly whereas the Maastricht Treaty had required that member countries keep their public debt below 60 percent of GDP, the Eurozone's peripheral countries have seen their public debt levels rise to well above 100 percent of GDP.

In addition to compromising their public finances, the peripheral countries have lost a great degree of external competitiveness as a result of relatively high domestic inflation.

This has contributed to very large external current account deficits in the periphery and very high external debt to GDP ratios.

Economic Imbalances in the European Periphery

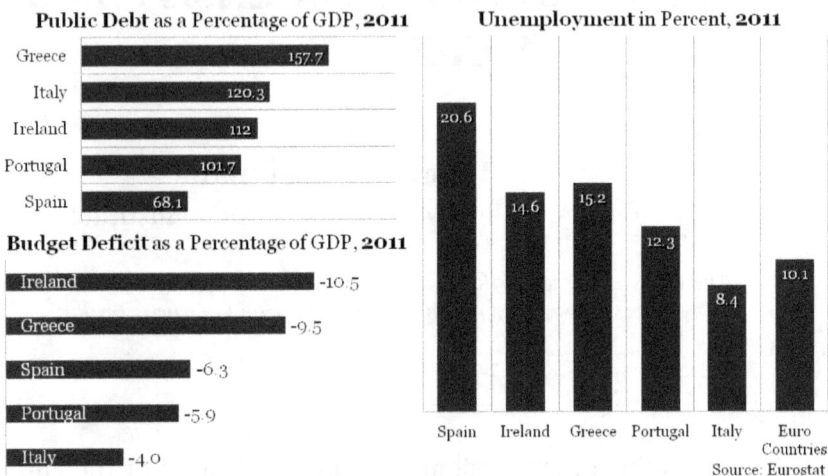

Public Debt as a Percentage of GDP, 2011

Greece 157.7
Italy 120.3
Ireland 112
Portugal 101.7
Spain 68.1

Budget Deficit as a Percentage of GDP, 2011

Ireland -10.5
Greece -9.5
Spain -6.3
Portugal -5.9
Italy -4.0

Unemployment in Percent, 2011

Spain 20.6
Ireland 14.6
Greece 15.2
Portugal 12.3
Italy 8.4
Euro Countries 10.1

Source: Eurostat

2. The essence of the peripheral countries' problem is that stuck within the Euro **they are not able to devalue their currencies as a means of boosting their exports.** Attempting to comply with the IMF-EU programs of massive fiscal austerity without the benefit of devaluation to redress their internal and external imbalances is producing very deep recessions in these countries. That in turn is eroding these countries' tax bases and is sapping those countries' political willingness to stay the IMF course. It is also not helping these countries reduce their very high public debt to GDP levels.

3. The seriousness of the present Eurozone debt crisis is that it has the potential for causing a full blown banking crisis in Europe's core countries. While the Eurozone periphery might not constitute a large part of the overall European economy, the peripheral countries are highly indebted. The total sovereign debt of Greece, Ireland, Portugal, and Spain is around US $2 trillion. A large part of that debt sits uncomfortably on the balance sheets of the French and the German banks.

The Euro Crisis is intensifying

4. Over the past few months, there has been **a marked intensification of the Eurozone debt crisis** that could have major implications for the United States economy in 2012. Among the signs of intensification are the following:

- The Greek economy now appears to be in virtual freefall as indicated by a 12 percent contraction in real GDP over the past two years and an increase in the unemployment rate to over 15 percent. This makes a substantial write-down of Greece's US $450 billion sovereign debt highly probable within the next few months. Such a default would constitute the largest sovereign debt default on record.

- Contagion from the Greek debt crisis is affecting not simply the smaller economies of Ireland and Portugal, which too have solvency problems. It is now also impacting Italy and Spain, Europe's third and fourth largest economies, respectively. This poses a real threat to the Euro's survival in its present form.

- The Eurozone debt crisis is having a material impact on the European banking system. This is being reflected in an approximate halving in European bank share prices and an increase in European banks' funding costs. French banks in particular are having trouble funding themselves in the wholesale bank market.

- There are very clear indications of an appreciable slowing in German and French economic growth. It is all too likely that the overall European economy could soon be tipped into a meaningful economic recession should there be a worsening in Europe's banking crisis. A worsening in the growth prospects of Europe's core countries reduces the chances that the countries in the European periphery can grow themselves out of their present debt crisis.

5. The IMF now acknowledges that Greece's economic and budget performance has been very much worse than anticipated and that **the Greek economy is basically insolvent.** The IMF

estimates that Greece's public debt to GDP ratio will rise to at least 180 percent or to a level that is clearly unsustainable. The IMF is proposing that the European banks accept a 50-60 cent on the dollar write-down on their Greek sovereign debt holding. This would have a material impact on the European banks' capital reserve positions.

6. The European Central Bank (ECB) is correctly warning that a Greek default would have a devastating effect on the Greek banking system, which has very large holdings of Greek sovereign debt. This could necessitate the imposition of capital controls or the nationalization of the Greek banking system. The ECB is also rightly fearful that **a Greek default will soon trigger similar debt defaults in Portugal and Ireland** since depositors in those countries might take fright following a Greek default. This has to be a matter of major concern since the combined sovereign debt of Greece, Portugal, and Ireland is around US $1 trillion.

7. Since July 2011, **the Italian and Spanish bond markets have been under substantial market pressure**. This has necessitated more than US $100 billion in ECB purchases of these countries' bonds in the secondary market. An intensification of contagion to Italy and Spain would pose an existential threat to the Euro in its present form given that the combined public debt of these two countries is currently around US$4 trillion.

8. While to a large degree European policymakers are right in portraying Italy and Spain as innocent bystanders to the Greek debt crisis, **Italy and Spain both have pronounced economic vulnerabilities**. Italy's public debt to GDP ratio is presently at an uncomfortably high 120 percent, while it suffers from both very sclerotic economic growth and a dysfunctional political system. For its part, Spain is presently saddled with a net external debt of around 100 percent of GDP, it still has a sizeable external current account deficit, and it is still in the process of adjusting to the bursting of a housing market bubble that was a multiple the size of that in the United States.

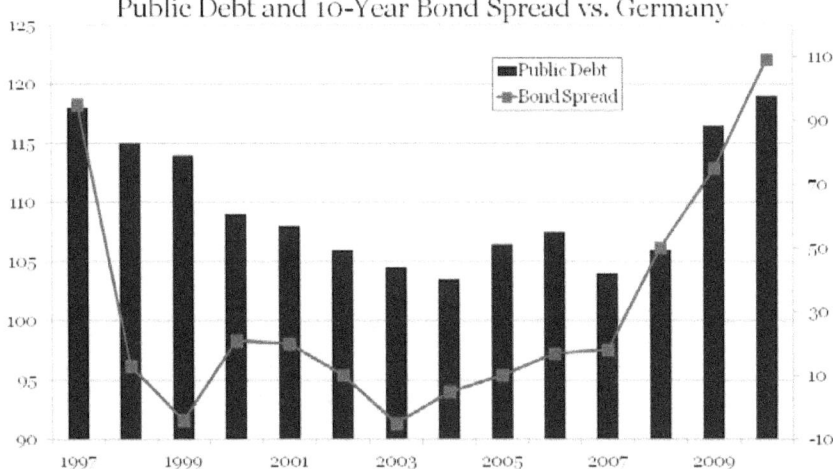

Italy's Public Debt is High

Public Debt and 10-Year Bond Spread vs. Germany

9. Sovereign debt defaults in the European periphery would have a major impact on the balance sheet position of the European banking system. The IMF estimates that **the European banks are presently undercapitalized** by around US $300 billion, while some private estimates consider that the banks are undercapitalized by more than US $400 billion. It is of concern to the European economic outlook that there are already signs of the European banks selling assets and constraining their lending to improve their capital ratios.

US and European Banks' CDS Spreads

Five-year credit default swap spreads in basis points

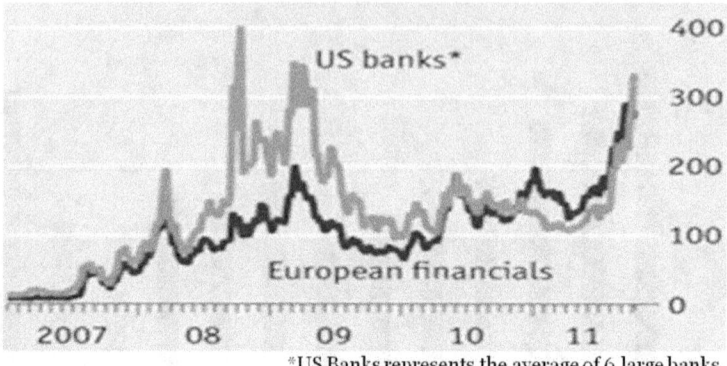

*US Banks represents the average of 6 large banks

Source: Markit, the Economist

Implications for the United States Economy

10. Considering that the European economy accounts for over 30 percent of global economic output, **a deepening of the European crisis could very well derail the US economic recovery**. In principle, a deepening in the European economic crisis could impact the US economy through three distinct channels:

- A renewed European economic recession would diminish US export prospects to an important market for US goods.

- A weakening in the Euro against the dollar, which would very likely flow from a European banking crisis and from questions about the Euro's survival in its present form, would put United States companies at a marked disadvantage with respect to European companies in third markets.

- In much the same way as the US Lehman crisis of 2008-2009 severely impacted the European economy through financial market dislocation, a European banking crisis would materially impact the US economy both through the financial market channel and through a generalized increase in global economic risk aversion.

11. Secretary of the Treasury Geithner has correctly asserted that the United States financial system has relatively limited direct exposure to the Greek, Irish, Portuguese, or Spanish economies. However, this assertion overlooks the fact that **the US financial system is hugely exposed to the European banking system**, which in turn is directly exposed to the European periphery. Among the indicators of this heavy exposure are the following:

- According to the Fitch rating agency, short-term loans by US money market funds to the European banking system still total over US $1 trillion or more than 40 percent of their total overall assets.
- According to the Bank for International Settlements, the US banks have exposure to the German and French economies in excess of US $1.2 trillion.
- According to BIS estimates, US banks have written derivative contracts on the sovereign debt of the European periphery in excess of US $400 billion.
- The recent Dexia bank failure in Belgium has revealed close interconnections between European and US banks.

What is to be done?

12. European policymakers are presently engaged in an effort to put forward **a comprehensive plan to address the crisis** ahead of the forthcoming G-20 Summit on November 3-4, 2011. After many months of denial, they now recognize the severity of Greece's solvency problem and the serious risks that a disorderly Greek default would pose to the European economy. The Plan that the Europeans announced on October 26, 2011 comprised the following three pillars:

- A revision to the IMF-EU program aimed at putting Greece's public finances on a sustainable path. The proposed revision would include the requirement that Greece's bank creditors accept a 50 percent write down on their Greek loans than the 21 percent haircut that was earlier agreed upon in July 2011.
- The erection of a credible firewall around Italy and Spain. By substantially leveraging up the European

Financial Stability Facility (EFSF), European policymakers hope to have at their disposal around US$1.4 trillion that could be used to purchase Italian and Spanish bonds.

- The recapitalization of the European banking system with a view to creating an adequate cushion for the European banks to absorb the losses from a Greek default.

13. Over the past eighteen months, the European policymakers' response to the Eurozone debt crisis has been one of "too little, too late" to get ahead of the crisis. There is the real risk that the efforts presently underway will also fall short of what is needed to finally defuse this crisis. Among the areas of concern are the following:

- It remains to be seen whether Greece's bank creditors will voluntarily accept the large debt write downs that are now being proposed by European policymakers. It is also concerning that even after the proposed debt write down Greece's public debt to GDP ratio would remain as high as 120 percent.
- It is not clear whether European policymakers will succeed in leveraging up the EFSF by a sufficient amount to reassure investors in Italian and Spanish bonds. Nor is it clear whether they will be able to do so in a manner that allows those resources to be readily used to effectively prop up the Italian and Spanish bond markets without excessive interference by the German Bundestag or without IMF conditionality.
- There is the danger that leaving it up to the banks to improve their capital over the next 9 months will result in increased bank asset sales and credit restrictions. This could result in an intensification of Europe's incipient credit crunch that would increase the odds that the European economy experiences a meaningful double dip recession.

The US Role in resolving the Crisis

14. To date, the **US has supported the Europeans through the IMF, in which the US has a 17 percent stake, and the through the Federal Reserve.** Over the past eighteen months, in each of the massive IMFEU bailout programs for Greece, Ireland, and Portugal, the IMF has provided around one third of the total funding. Meanwhile, the US Federal Reserve has made amply available to the European Central Bank large amounts of US dollar funding through enhanced US dollar swap lines.

15. A number of considerations would suggest that beyond exhorting European policymakers to be more decisive of their handling of the crisis **there is little more that the United States should be doing** to support the Europeans in resolving their crisis. Among these considerations are the following:

- The essence of the problem confronting Greece, Ireland, and Portugal is one of solvency rather than one of liquidity. Providing additional funding to these countries to essentially help them kick the can down the road does little to resolve these countries' solvency problems.
- Providing funding to help prop up the Italian and Spanish sovereign bond markets would be putting US taxpayers' money at risk given the troubled economic fundamentals of these two countries.
- In light of the United States own budgetary problems, it is not clear why additional US taxpayers' money should be used to either bailout countries in the European periphery or to support European banks. It would seem that much in the same way as the US did not seek European support to help it resolve the 2009 US banking sector crisis, the Europeans should now use their own budget resources to resolve their own sovereign debt and banking crises.

Statement before the Senate Committee on Foreign Affairs
Subcommittee on Europe and Eurasia
The European Debt Crisis: Strategic Implications for the

Transatlantic Alliance
The Eurozone Debt Crisis and the United States
November 2, 2011

"Dear Secretary Geithner"

By
Mark Kirk
Republican U.S. Senator of Illinois

Following the failure of European leaders to build decisive consensus on managing the growing European sovereign debt crisis, U.S. Senator Mark Kirk (R-IL) wrote to Treasury Secretary Geithner about the 'systemic risk' this crisis poses to U.S. banks and other financial institutions.

Under the 2010 Wall Street Reform and Consumer Protection Act, a new 'Financial Stability Oversight Council' must review and mitigate 'systemic risks' that could threaten U.S. banks or other financial institutions. Sen. Kirk, a junior member of the Senate Banking Committee, called on Secretary Geithner, the Chairman of the new Council, to conduct a "thorough analysis of the risk posed to U.S. financial institutions by the European sovereign debt crisis".

According to the non-partisan Congressional Research Service, the European countries in crisis (Greece, Portugal, Spain, Ireland and Italy) directly owe U.S. banks $180.9 billion and are exposed to a further $586.6 billion in indirect risks posed by this crisis. Senator Kirk wrote, "events are moving so quickly that real-time, dynamic oversight of the European sovereign debt crisis needs to be a FSOC priority right now". The letter also referenced Fitch Ratings warning that the U.S. banking industry faces "serious risk" and the Federal Reserve Bank of San Francisco warning that, "a European sovereign debt default may well sink the United States back into recession."

The full text of the letter:

December 12, 2011

Dear Secretary Geithner:

The Financial Stability Oversight Council (FSOC) was established to monitor emerging threats to the stability of the financial system and identify risks in U.S. financial institutions. Additionally, the Office of Financial Research (OFR) was created to assist the Council in collecting the necessary data to assess systemic risk. The European sovereign debt crisis could now pose a systemic risk to the U.S. financial system and warrants enhanced monitoring by FSOC.

In recent months, U.S. financial markets experienced significant volatility. Many shocks in equities and bond valuations were related to developments in the Euro-zone. We have already witnessed one firm, MF Global Inc., file for bankruptcy as a result of over-exposure to European sovereign debt. Fitch Ratings warned that the U.S. banking industry faces "serious risk" from the European sovereign debt crisis. The Federal Reserve Bank of San Francisco tells us, "a European sovereign debt default may well sink the United States back into recession."

With multiple signals that the crisis in the Euro-zone does indeed present a risk to the U.S. economy and financial sector, what monitoring and research is FSOC undertaking or requiring covered financial institutions to conduct to assess this systemic risk? Certainly, the Bank for International Settlements and the Depository Trust & Clearing Corporation provide data that can be compiled to show U.S. financial exposure on a static basis. However, events are moving so quickly that real-time, dynamic oversight of the European sovereign debt crisis needs to be a FSOC priority right now.

In 2011, FSOC reported on concentration limits on large financial companies, secured creditor haircuts and the Volcker Rule. The S&P Credit Watch warning against European sovereign debt has the potential to eclipse the risks of the other subjects examined by the Council. This is the type of research and analysis that I believe FSOC must undertake and make publicly available.

Sincerely,

Mark Kirk
United States Senator

What the Crisis Means for Taxpayers and the U.S. Economy

By
William Dudley
President Federal Reserve Bank of New York

The views expressed do not represent official views of the Federal Reserve Board, the Federal Open Market Committee ("FOMC") or any other part of the Federal Reserve System.

The Federal Reserve seeks to promote financial stability in order to enable U.S. businesses and households to maintain their access to credit and to ensure sustained economic growth. Although the U.S. economy is currently expanding at a moderate pace, we face significant downside risks, mostly relating to the sovereign debt crisis in Europe. Because developments in Europe will have an important bearing on the prospects for growth and jobs here in the U.S., the Federal Reserve is monitoring the situation there closely. This is also why we have taken special steps, in cooperation with other central banks, to support the flow of credit to households and businesses.

Europe

Within the European Union, seventeen countries share a common currency, the euro. The situation in the euro area is very unsettled, with pressure on sovereign debt markets and local banking systems. The euro area has the capacity, including the fiscal capacity, to overcome its challenges. However, the politics are very difficult, both because the problem has many dimensions, and because many different countries and institutions in the euro area have to coordinate their actions in order to achieve a coherent and effective policy response.

Europe's leadership has affirmed its commitment to the European Union and its single currency monetary union on numerous occasions. And the leadership is working to achieve greater policy coordination in areas such as fiscal policy. Putting all the countries using the euro on a clearly sustainable fiscal path would help restore market confidence. Assuming that Europe ultimately succeeds in managing this situation, a stronger union will emerge that will be viewed as more robust and resilient. This would be a welcome development for the U.S.

If, in contrast, Europe were not to be fully successful in charting an effective course, this could have a number of negative implications for the U.S.

First, if the European situation were to deteriorate, then the euro area would face even more serious fiscal and economic challenges. As a result, growth within the euro zone would weaken and this would lead to less demand for U.S. goods and services that are exported to Europe from companies and workers here. This would hurt growth here in the United States and would have a negative impact on U.S. jobs. It is important to recognize that the euro area is the world's second largest economy after the U.S. and an important trading partner for us. Also, Europe is a significant investor in the U.S. economy, and vice versa. Thus, what happens in Europe has significant implications for our economy.

Second, if the European situation were to deteriorate, this could put pressure on the U.S. banking system. The good news is that U.S. banks are much more robust and resilient than they were a few years ago. U.S. banks have bolstered their capital significantly, built up their loan loss reserves, and have significantly larger liquidity buffers. Also, the direct exposures of U.S. banks to the countries in Europe that are facing the most intense fiscal challenges are actually quite modest.

The bad news is that the exposures of the U.S. banks climb quite sharply when one also considers the exposures to the core European countries and to the overall European banking system. This means that if the crisis were to broaden further and intensify, this could put greater pressure on U.S. banks' capital and liquidity buffers.

Third, if the European situation were to deteriorate further, financial markets would likely become more stressed. This could tighten the availability of credit to U.S. households and businesses. It could also cause equity prices to fall and this would have a negative impact on Americans' pension and 401(k) holdings. This tightening of financial conditions would damage the U.S. recovery and result in slower output growth and less job creation. At a time that U.S. unemployment is very high, this is a particularly unacceptable outcome. In the extreme, U.S. financial markets could become so impaired that this would dry up the flow of credit to households and businesses.

U.S. Dollar Swaps

In terms of what actions the official sector in the United States has taken or could take with regard to Europe, I wish to emphasize that any and all such actions pursued by the Federal Reserve are motivated by the mandates Congress has given to the Federal Reserve to promote price stability and maximum sustainable employment here in the United States.

When the Federal Reserve System was created by Congress in 1913, it was given the responsibility of providing liquidity to the financial system in times of stress in order to shield the economy, to the extent possible, from the severe effects of financial instability on economic activity and jobs. While the economy and the markets have evolved substantially in the century since then, this basic principle continues to guide our efforts today. Central banks around the world have an important lender of last resort role. This role is important in order to protect the economy against financial instability.

In today's globally integrated economy, banks headquartered outside of the U.S. play an important role in providing credit and other financial services in the U.S. - providing a total of about $900 billion in overall financing within the U.S. For these banks to provide U.S. dollar loans, they have to maintain access to U.S. dollar funding. At a time when it is already hard enough for American families and firms to get the credit they need, we have a strong interest in making sure that these banks can continue to be active in the U.S. dollar markets.

Banks headquartered outside the U.S., like banks that are headquartered here, make extensive use of dollars in their financing activities. In part, this is due to the fact that the U.S. dollar is the world's number one currency - a status that brings with it many benefits for our country. It is in the U.S. national interest to make sure that non-U.S. banks that are judged to be sound by their central bank are able to access the U.S. dollar funding they need in order to be able to continue to finance their U.S. dollar assets. If the access to dollar funding were severely impaired, this could necessitate the abrupt, forced sales of dollar assets by these banks, which could seriously disrupt U.S. markets and adversely affect U.S. businesses, consumers, and jobs.

One way we can help to support the availability of dollar funding is by engaging in currency swaps with other central banks. This has been used as a policy tool dating back to 1962. Recently, the Federal Open Market Committee decided to re-launch this tool, cooperating with five other central banks. Our intention is to create a credible backstop to - but not supplant -

private markets. Banks with surplus dollars are more likely to lend to banks in need of dollars if they know that the borrowing bank will be able to obtain the dollars it needs to repay the loan, if necessary, from its central bank.

This action is designed to support financial stability, avoid an unnecessary tightening in financial conditions, and support economic activity and jobs in the United States. In particular, by reducing the cost of dollar funding via the swap lines last month, we reduced the pressure on banks in Europe to abruptly liquidate their U.S. dollar assets. Thus, this step will help to insulate
U.S. markets from the pressures in Europe and support the availability of credit to U.S. households and businesses. European banks are particularly active in areas such as trade finance, project finance, energy lending and municipal finance – a sharp contraction of the financing they provide would be harmful for the U.S. economy as a whole, including for U.S. exporters, firms working on infrastructure projects, the energy industry and hard-pressed state and local governments across the country.

U.S. financial institutions currently do not face difficulty obtaining liquidity in short-term funding markets. However, were conditions to deteriorate, the Federal Reserve has a range of tools available to provide an effective liquidity backstop for such institutions and is prepared to use these tools as needed to support financial stability and to promote the extension of credit to U.S. households and businesses.

The Federal Reserve is actively and carefully assessing this situation and the potential impact on the U.S. economy. At this time, although I do not anticipate further efforts by the Federal Reserve to address the potential spillover effects of Europe on the United States, we will continue to monitor the situation closely.

Testimony of before the
Subcommittee on TARP, Financial Services and
Bailouts of Public and Private Programs
of the
Committee on Oversight and Government Reform
U.S. House of Representatives

December 16, 2011

What the Crisis Means for Taxpayers and the U.S. Economy

By
Steven B. Kamin
Director Division of International Finance Board of Governors of
the Federal Reserve System

For two years now, the tone of global financial markets has become progressively more entangled with fiscal and financial developments in Europe. The combination of high debt levels and low growth prospects in several European countries using the euro has raised concerns about their fiscal sustainability. Such concerns were initially focused on Greece but have since spread to other euro-area countries, leading to substantial increases in their sovereign borrowing costs. Pessimism about their fiscal situation, in turn, has helped to undermine confidence in the strength of European financial institutions, increasing their cost of raising funds and threatening to curtail their supply of credit. These developments have placed significant strains on global financial markets and have weighed on global economic activity.

Late last week, European leaders announced new steps to address the crisis, including proposals to strengthen fiscal rules and European fiscal coordination, as well as to enhance and provide additional clarity on the timing and design of a more credible euro-area financial backstop. These steps are a positive development and indicate the commitment of European leaders to alleviate the crisis. However, many key details of their proposed policies have yet to be worked out, and implementing them will be a challenge. Hence, it will be critical for European authorities to follow through on their commitments in the days and weeks ahead.

Here at home, the financial stresses in Europe are undoubtedly spilling over to the United States by restraining our exports, helping to push down business and consumer confidence, and adding to pressures on U.S. financial markets and institutions. Of note, foreign financial institutions, especially those in Europe, are finding it more difficult to fund themselves in dollars.

A great deal of trade and investment the world over is financed in dollars, so many foreign financial institutions have heavy borrowing needs in our currency. These institutions also borrow heavily in dollars because they are active in U.S. markets, purchasing government and corporate securities as well as making loans to households and firms. As concerns about the financial system in Europe have mounted, many European banks have faced a rise in the cost and decline in the availability of dollar funding. Difficulty acquiring dollar funding by European and other financial institutions may ultimately make it harder and more costly for U.S. households and businesses to get loans. Moreover, these disruptions could spill over into the market for borrowing and lending in U.S. dollars more generally, raising the cost of funding for U.S. financial institutions. Although the breadth and size of all of these effects on the U.S. economy are difficult to gauge, the situation in Europe poses a significant risk to U.S. economic activity and bears close watching.

Swap Lines with Other Central Banks

To address these potential risks to the United States, the Federal Reserve agreed with the European Central Bank (ECB) and the central banks of Canada, Japan, Switzerland, and the United Kingdom to revise, extend, and expand its swap lines with these institutions. 1 These actions were described in a joint announcement by the Federal Reserve and the other central banks on November 30. The measures were motivated by the need to ease strains in global financial markets, which, if left unchecked, could impair the supply of credit to households and businesses in the United States and impede our economic recovery. At present, such strains are particularly evident in Europe, and these actions were designed to help prevent disruptions in financial markets there from spilling over to the U.S. economy.

Three steps were described in the November 30 announcement. First, we reduced the pricing of drawings on the dollar liquidity swap lines. The previous pricing had been at a spread of 100 basis points over the overnight index swap rate.2 We reduced that spread to 50 basis points. The lower cost to the ECB and other foreign central banks will enable them to reduce the cost of the dollar loans they provide to financial institutions in their jurisdictions. Reducing these costs should help alleviate pressures in U.S. money markets generated by foreign financial institutions, strengthen the liquidity positions of European and other foreign institutions, and boost confidence at a time of considerable strains in international financial markets. Through all of these channels, the action should help support the continued supply of credit to U.S. households and businesses.

Second, we extended the authorization for these lines through February 1, 2013. The previous authorization had been through August 1, 2012. This extension demonstrates that central banks are prepared to work together for a sustained period, if needed, to support global liquidity conditions.

Third, we agreed to establish, as a precautionary measure, swap lines in the currencies of the other central banks participating in the announcement. (The Federal Reserve had established similar lines in April 2009, but they were not drawn upon and were allowed to expire in February 2010.) Once such lines are set up, the Federal Reserve could, if needed, activate one or more of these lines and draw foreign currencies. With such access to foreign currency funds, the Federal Reserve could provide euros, Canadian dollars, Japanese yen, Swiss francs, or British pounds to U.S. financial institutions on a secured basis, much as the foreign central banks provide dollars to institutions in their jurisdictions now. U.S. financial institutions are not experiencing any foreign currency liquidity pressures at present, but we judged it prudent to make arrangements to offer such liquidity should the need arise in the future.

I would like to emphasize that information on the swap lines is fully disclosed on the Federal Reserve's website--through the weekly balance sheet release and other materials--and information on swap transactions each week is provided on the website of the Federal Reserve Bank of New York.3

I also want to underscore that these swap agreements are safe from the perspective of the Federal Reserve and the U.S. taxpayer:

- First, the swap transactions themselves present no exchange rate or interest rate risk to the Fed. Because the terms of each drawing and repayment are set at the time that the draw is initiated, fluctuations in exchange rates and interest rates that may occur while the swap funds are outstanding do not alter the eventual repayments.

- Second, each drawing on the swap line must be approved by the Federal Reserve, which allows the Federal Reserve to monitor use of the facility by the foreign central banks.
- Third, the foreign currency held by the Federal Reserve during the term of the swap provides an important safeguard.
- Fourth, our counterparties in these swap agreements are the foreign central banks. In turn, it is they who lend the dollars they draw from the swap lines to private institutions in their own jurisdictions. The foreign central banks assume the credit risk associated with lending to these institutions. The Federal Reserve has had long and close relationships with these central banks, and our interactions with them over the years have provided a track record that justifies a high degree of trust and cooperation.
- Finally, the short tenor of the swap drawings, which have maturities of at most three months, also offers some protection, in that positions could be wound down relatively quickly were it judged appropriate to do so

The Federal Reserve has not lost a penny on any of the swap line transactions since these lines were established in 2007, even during the most intense period of activity at the end of 2008. Moreover, at the maturity of each swap transaction, the Federal Reserve receives the dollars it provided plus a fee. These fees have added roughly $6 billion to overall earnings on Federal Reserve operations over the past five years, thereby increasing the amount the Federal Reserve has returned to taxpayers.

Conclusion

The implementation of the changes in swap arrangements has had some positive effects on dollar funding markets. On the announcement of the changes, several measures of the cost of dollar funding declined. Moreover, at the auctions of three-month dollar funding conducted by our foreign central bank counterparties the following week, the amount of dollars provided escalated substantially.

---

1 See Board of Governors of the Federal Reserve System (2011), "Coordinated Central Bank Action to Address Pressures in Global Money Markets," press release, November 30,
   www.federalreserve.gov/newsevents/press/monetary/20111130a.htm.

2 The dollar overnight index swap rate is the fixed rate that one party agrees to pay in exchange for the average of the overnight federal funds rates over the life of the swap. As such, it is a measure of the average federal funds rate expected over the term of the swap.

3 For each week's Federal Reserve balance sheet, see www.federalreserve.gov/releases/h41. For other relevant information and materials on the Federal Reserve's website, see www.federalreserve.gov/monetarypolicy/bst_liquidityswaps.htm. For weekly information on the Federal Reserve's swap transactions with other central banks, see www.newyorkfed.org/markets/fxswap/fxswap.cfm. Finally, for copies of the agreements between the Federal Reserve and other central banks, as well as other information, see www.newyorkfed.org/markets/liquidity_swap.html.

Before the Subcommittee on TARP, Financial Services
and
Bailouts of Public and Private Programs
Committee on Oversight and Government Reform
U.S. House of Representatives
December 16, 2011

What the Crisis Means for Taxpayers and the U.S. Economy

By
Mark Sobel
Deputy Assistant Secretary

The European Economic Outlook is Weakening

Over the past year, economic and financial stresses in Europe have spread to some of Europe's largest economies, and the crisis now facing Europe is deeper and more entrenched. Sovereign bond yields have risen sharply in many countries. Many European financial institutions have faced difficulties in obtaining funding from markets and are de-leveraging in order to strengthen their capital adequacy. European equities have fallen by a quarter since April.

These developments have resulted in a sharp weakening in Europe's current growth performance and significant markdowns in growth projections for 2012. Growth in the euro area is projected by most analysts to be negative this quarter and into early 2012, with weak growth persisting in 2012. For example, the OECD, which earlier this year had projected annual average European growth in 2012 of 2.0 percent, just revised its estimate to 0.2 percent. Many private forecasters are more pessimistic.

Europe's problems are a serious risk for the U.S. outlook
In the United States, the pace of recovery has strengthened recently and most analysts expect continued moderate growth

next year. But given Europe's strong trade and financial linkages with the rest of the world, other regions could feel the impact as well. Indeed, Europe's problems are a serious risk for the U.S. economic outlook.

· The European Union buys nearly 20 percent of U.S. goods exports ($242.6 billion in 2010) and over 30 percent of U.S. service exports ($170.2 billion). The European Union accounts for 63 percent of the stock of foreign direct investment (FDI) into the United States, at $1.5 trillion, and 56 percent of new investment in 2010. Therefore, when European growth slows, U.S. jobs, exports, and FDI inflows decline.

· Global financial markets are strongly interconnected. When European financial markets tighten, it can adversely impact U.S. banks' confidence and their willingness to lend and invest. That, in turn, can hurt American businesses and jobs, particularly in smaller firms that depend on credit from their banks to grow and innovate.

· When EU stocks decline, U.S. equity markets often do as well, hitting the savings and wealth of Americans.

To make these linkages more concrete, for instance, exports to the European Union represent over 24, 20 and 18 percent, respectively, of merchandise exports from New York, North Carolina, and Illinois. In each of these states, over 150,000 jobs – and over 250,000 in Illinois – are export-related. A decline in exports to Europe will inevitably adversely impact America.

Engaging Europe

First and foremost, Europe has an enormous self-interest in tackling its problems. The events of the last two years have highlighted the need for the currency union to have an adequate crisis response toolkit to respond to economic and financial stress, as well as stronger disciplines to assure long-term fiscal and external sustainability. As President Obama and Secretary Geithner have stated on numerous occasions, Europe clearly has the capacity and the resources to address its crisis.

Europe is making progress in putting in place reforms to create the conditions for future economic growth and to build a stronger architecture for fiscal union. The recent European Council agreement represents an important step forward. But more work remains to be done.

Our ties to Europe are deep and longstanding. The Transatlantic partnership is vital to our national security.

Supporting Europe is not just a matter of diplomacy or friendship. Rather, it is a matter of vital national interest for the well being of the American economy, for the wellbeing of American workers, for the wellbeing of American businesses, and for the wellbeing of American families and individuals saving for their future.

Therefore, we are heavily engaged with Europe through bilateral and multilateral channels.

Bilaterally, the President is actively engaged. There are extensive contacts with European leaders. Secretary Geithner has traveled to Europe 3 times in the last 3 months to engage with his counterparts. Over the past two years, we have offered our perspective about the dangers that the sovereign debt crisis poses for the global recovery. And we have shared the lessons from our own financial crisis, including the importance of responding to market challenges decisively and with overwhelming force.

Multilaterally we are working closely with countries around the world to help promote a stronger and more balanced global economy. To do so, we have valuable international fora, particularly the G-20—which is the principal forum for international economic and financial cooperation with membership comprising 85 percent of the global economy—and the International Monetary Fund (IMF or Fund).

Recognizing the strong linkages among their economies, G-20 Leaders underscored at the London Summit in April 2009 their willingness to aggressively tackle and stabilize the global economy and financial system. Together, they undertook a massive and powerful cooperative effort. Later that year in Pittsburgh, with global economic conditions steadying and the recovery underway, Leaders agreed on a Framework for Strong, Sustainable and Balanced Growth that requires actions by all G-20 countries to address the global imbalances that preceded the crisis.

The world's ability to tackle its medium term challenges will require cooperative actions by all, but it surely also requires tackling and overcoming the near term challenges. This, in turn, underscores the significance of an effective European response to the euro area crisis. Last month in Cannes, France, G-20 Leaders focused heavily on the European crisis. The Cannes Summit Communiqué underscored the importance of strengthening European banks, building an effective European firewall to avoid contagion, and laying the foundations for robust economic governance reform in the euro area. Mexico will chair the G-20 in 2012, and it already has stressed that promoting a more effective European crisis response will be a top priority.

The IMF is a central institution of the international monetary system, and international monetary cooperation is as vital today as it was when the IMF was founded over sixty years ago. Throughout this time period, the Fund has served well the global community and U.S. economic interests. It helped Europe and Japan achieve sustained growth in the post-war period. After the demise of the Bretton Woods System, it helped the U.K. and Italy overcome their crises in the 1970s, resolve the Latin American debt crisis of the 1980s, support economic transition in Eastern Europe and the former Soviet Union in the 1990s, and was central to the response to the Asian and emerging market financial crisis late in the 1990s and earlier this decade.

Secretaries Baker, Brady, Bentsen, Rubin, Summers, O'Neill, Snow, Paulson, and Geithner all stand squarely behind the IMF as it addresses the most critical financial and economic challenges of our times. Through this support, the United States has been able to exercise strong global leadership in responding to crises.

The Fund has not wavered in its belief in the central role of sound economic policies and reforms, but it has responded with flexibility to the needs of countries. Countries first and foremost bear the burden of adjustment. They must put their fiscal houses in order and live within their means. But the Fund can play a role in promoting more orderly adjustment by offering financing to support economic reforms, thereby providing some breathing space to countries in overcoming their problems in ways that are less disruptive.

When growth plummets in one country, especially a large country, it spills over onto others. In these circumstances, the Fund's support also helps mitigate the impact on innocent bystanders and the system as a whole. The global financial crisis in 2009 is a good example. Numerous emerging market economies, including many that had strengthened their performance over the prior decade and were engines of growth for the world economy, were hit by a massive outflow of capital that threatened to undermine their hard-won gains. The actions taken by national authorities in early 2009, coupled in particular with the announcement at the London Summit of new and significant support for the IMF, helped stem the capital outflows and steady the international financial system. This action was pivotal in promoting global recovery.

The IMF is a very good investment for the United States. The Fund helps promote global stability and lessen the fallout from events abroad to American workers and families. When the Fund lends, it does so subject to appropriate conditions and with safeguards to assure it is repaid. And its repayment record is outstanding. When the IMF draws on U.S. resources, the United States is exposed to the Fund's balance sheet - not the borrowing countries - and the Fund's balance sheet is rock solid. The Fund is regarded as the world's preferred creditor, meaning that the IMF's member countries acknowledge and agree that it gets repaid first.

The Role of the Fund in Europe

The crisis in Europe is severe, and it is impacting not only Europe, but the entire global economy. The challenge Europe faces, however, is completely within the capacity of the stronger European members to manage. As European countries act to develop critical economic reforms and to strengthen fiscal governance, Europe must also continue mobilizing the requisite resources to put in place a strong and credible firewall commensurate with the scale of the challenge. It must do so quickly, with force and determination.

The United States and our international partners stand with European leaders as they move to put in place decisive solutions. The IMF is important in providing external assessments of reform programs which have unparalleled credibility. The IMF cannot substitute for a strong and credible European firewall and response.

The IMF now has a substantial arsenal of financial resources – almost $400 billion. The Administration has been clear with our international partners that we have no intention of seeking additional funding for the IMF.

Conclusion

Our nation's economic recovery and job creation depend on a strong world economy and stable international financial markets. The global economy now faces deep challenges that threaten domestic and global growth and heighten financial instability. Foremost is the situation in Europe. Stresses that harm U.S.-European trade and propagate financial contagion from Europe adversely affect U.S. businesses, slow our recovery, and harm U.S. workers, jobs, and families. Let us work together, with our allies, and through our leadership in international fora and institutions, to overcome these challenges that put our recovery, and the world's, at risk.

Testimony of Mark Sobel
Before the House Oversight Subcommittee on
TARP, Financial Services and Bailouts of Public and Private Programs
December 16, 2011

APPENDIX A

Glossary of Terms Term

- **Definition Broad Economic Policy Guidelines (BEPG)** The *Broad Economic Policy Guidelines (BEPGs)* are adopted by the Council as a reference document guiding the conduct of the whole range of economic policies in the Member States and the European Union. They play a central role in the system of economic policy coordination, setting out economic policy recommendations which give a basis for economic policy in both the Member States and the EU as a whole in the current year.
- **Council of the European Union ("Council of Ministers" or "Council")** The *Council of the European Union* is the Union's main decision-making body and enacts legislation based on proposals from the European Commission. Its meetings are attended by the member state ministers, and is thus the institution which represents the member states. The Presidency of the Council rotates among the member states every six months.
- **Economic and Monetary Union (EMU)** *Economic and Monetary Union* (EMU) is the process of harmonizing the economic and monetary policies of the member states of the European Union with a view to the introduction of a single currency, the euro.
- **European Central Bank (ECB)** Founded on June 30, 1998, the *European Central Bank* (ECB) is the institution of the European Union responsible for setting the monetary policy of the 16 EU member states taking part in the Eurozone. The bank is headquartered in Frankfurt, Germany.

- **European Commission (EC)** *The European Commission* (EC) acts as the EU's executive branch, and has the right of legislative initiative. There are 27 Commissioners—one from each country.
- **European Council** The *European Council* brings together the leaders of the member states and the Commission President. It acts as a strategic guide and driving force for EU policy.
- **European Financial Stability Facility (EFSF)** The *European Financial Stability Facility* (EFSF) was set up by the 16 Eurozone countries to provide a funding backstop should a euro area Member State find itself in financial difficulties. The EFSF has the capacity to issue bonds guaranteed by euro area members for up to € 440 billion in lending to Eurozone countries.
- **European Financial Stability Mechanism (EFSM)** The European Financial Stability Mechanism (EFSM) is a new €60 billion supranational EU balance of payments loan facility available to any EU member country facing financial difficulties.
- **The European System of Central Banks (ESCB)** The European System of Central Banks (ESCB) comprises the European Central Bank and the national central banks of all EU member states whether they have adopted the euro or not.
- **European Union (EU)** The *European Union* (EU) was established by the Treaty on European Union (Maastricht, 1992). The project of creating a Union has a long history, and was first mooted at the European Summit of 1972. The Union is both a political project and a form of legal organization.
- **Eurozone** The *Eurozone*, officially the *euro area*, is an economic and monetary union (EMU) of 17 EU members states which have adopted the euro currency as their sole legal tender. Monetary policy of the zone is the sole responsibility of the European Central Bank, though there is no common representation, governance or fiscal policy for the currency union. Some cooperation does, however, take place through the euro group,

which makes political decisions regarding the Eurozone and the euro.

- **Excessive Deficit Procedure (EDP)** The excessive deficit procedure is governed by Article 104 of the Treaty establishing the European Community, under which member states are obliged to avoid excessive deficits in national budgets.

- **Lisbon Treaty** The *Lisbon Treaty*, the latest institutional reform treaty of the European Union (EU), went into effect on December 1, 2009. It seeks to give the EU a stronger and more coherent voice with the creation of a new position, President of the European Council. It also makes changes to the EU's internal decision-making mechanisms, and foreign policy apparatus, among other provisions.

- **Maastricht Treaty** *The Treaty of Maastricht,* formally, the *Treaty on European Union* (TEU), was signed on February 7, 1992 by members of the European Community in Maastricht, Netherlands. Upon its entry into force on November 1, 1993, it created the European Union and led to the creation of the single European currency, the euro.

- **Sovereign debt** Sovereign debt is a financial liability of a national government.

- **Stability and Growth Pact (SGP)** The *Stability and Growth Pact* (SGP) pertains to the third stage of economic and monetary union (EMU), which began on January 1,1999. It is intended to ensure that member states maintain budgetary discipline after the single currency has been introduced.

Source: Europa Glossary
http://europa.eu/scadplus/glossary/index-en.html).

APPENDIX B

Background on the European Union

Following World War II, traditional European rivals sought to solidify peace by bringing their nations together under a common institutional structure. Influenced by his compatriot Jean Monnet, French Foreign Minister Robert Schuman officially tabled a plan on May 9, 1950 to pool French and German coal and steel production under an organization that would be open to other European countries. German Chancellor Konrad Adenauer supported this proposal, and six founding countries - Belgium, France, Germany, Italy, Luxembourg and the Netherlands - took an early step toward European integration by establishing the European Coal and Steel Community (ECSC) the following year.

After failing to establish a European Defense Community in the 1950s, the six countries then decided to set up a common market. With the entry into force of the Treaty of Rome in 1957, they created the European Economic Community (EEC), with an objective of liberating the movement of goods, capital, workers and services. (The European Atomic Energy Community (EURATOM) was also established at this time.) The Treaty of Rome established the basic institutions and decision-making mechanisms still in place in today's European Union. As of July 1, 1968, the EEC abolished customs duties between Member States on manufactured goods. New policies, including a common agricultural policy (CAP) and a common trade policy, were in place by the end of the 1960s.

The success of the European integration project during a period of steady economic growth in the 1960s set the stage for a first enlargement - the accession of the UK, Ireland and Denmark - in 1973. Further "deepening" of European integration followed: the Community acquired executive authority in social, regional, and environment policies. The benefits of economic convergence became more evident in the context of the 1970s energy crisis and financial turmoil, which led to the launch of the European Monetary System in 1979. In the same year, the first direct elections to the European Parliament (EP) took place. Previously, delegates from national parliaments had represented their country's legislative bodies at the EP in Strasbourg, France.

The Community further expanded southward with the accession of Greece (1981, the second enlargement), followed by Spain and Portugal (1986, the third enlargement). These accessions led the EEC to adopt "structural programs" in order to reduce economic and social disparities among its regions.

During the 1960s and 1970s, the Community began to assert itself on the international scene with the conclusion of agreements with southern Mediterranean countries. Starting in 1963, the EEC signed four successive Lome Conventions, which guaranteed trading advantages and development aid for Member States' former colonies in Africa, the Caribbean, and the Pacific (ACP).

World recession and internal disputes over Member States' financial burdens gave way, from 1985 onward, to renewed efforts for economic integration, enshrined in the 1985 "Single European Act" (SEA) and marked by the 1992 "Single Market Project." The SEA set January 1, 1993 as the date by which an internal single market was to be established and, by extending the practice of majority voting rather than unanimity in the EU Council, gave Community institutions the means of adopting the 300 Community-wide Directives required to abolish the remaining barriers and obstacles to intra-Community trade. In 1995, the Community entered into the "Barcelona" partnership with twelve southern Mediterranean countries. The partnership, reinforced by agreements on social, cultural, and human cooperation, was intended to lead to a free-trade area.

The collapse of the Berlin Wall and German unification prompted Member States to negotiate the 1992 Treaty on European Union (the "Maastricht Treaty"). In addition to establishing the European Union, the Maastricht Treaty set an ambitious program of further integration: establishment of Economic and Monetary Union (EMU) by 1999 (part of the "First or 'Community' Pillar"), setting up of a Common Foreign and Security Policy (CFSP) ("Second Pillar"); and cooperation on Justice and Home Affairs (JHA) ("Third Pillar"). Shortly thereafter, in 1995, Austria, Finland and Sweden joined the EU - the fourth enlargement.

Signed in 1997 and entering into force on May 1, 1999, the Amsterdam Treaty partially streamlined the EU institutional structure. Its most significant effects were: (1) to transfer aspects

The European Debt Crisis

of Justice and Home Affairs policy to the Community Pillar, enabling the Commission to propose decisions to be taken by the EU Council by qualified majority voting instead of by consensus, and (2) to establish a High Representative for the CFSP (who also serves as Secretary-General of the Council Secretariat). Ten countries in Central and Eastern Europe and Cyprus began accession procedures in 1997, followed by Malta. The prospect of eastward enlargement raised significant resource concerns and prompted the adoption in March 1999 of the "Agenda 2000" package, which covered amendments to the CAP and EU structural policies, as well as a budgetary framework through 2006.

In May 1998, EU heads of government officially designated eleven Member States eligible to adopt a single currency. Greece initially did not qualify, and Sweden, the UK and Denmark "opted out." On January 1, 1999, the euro became the official currency of the EU, and the European Central Bank (ECB) put euro notes and coins into circulation on January 1, 2002. Today, thirteen countries use the euro: Austria, Belgium, Finland, France, Germany, Greece, Ireland, Italy, Luxembourg, the Netherlands, Portugal, Slovenia, and Spain.

Streamlining the size and procedures of EU institutions to make the expanded EU more efficient was also an aim of the 2003 Treaty of Nice. A year later, in May 2004, Cyprus, the Czech Republic, Estonia, Hungary, Latvia, Lithuania, Malta, Poland, Slovakia, and Slovenia joined the EU, bringing total membership to 25. In 2007, Bulgaria and Romania joined the EU, which currently stands at 27 members. Formal Candidate countries currently include Turkey and Croatia, as well as the Republic of Macedonia.

In October 2004, Member States signed an EU Constitutional Treaty in Rome, intending that it take effect on November 1, 2006. French and Dutch voters rejected the treaty through referenda in 2005, thereby suspending the ratification process. A new effort, undertaken in June 2007, calls for the creation of an Intergovernmental Conference to form a political agreement, known as the Reform Treaty. In contrast to the Constitutional Treaty, the Reform Treaty would amend existing treaties rather than replace them. The IGC approved the new reform treaty, called the Lisbon Treaty, in October 2007. The Lisbon Treaty must be ratified by all 27 national Parliaments. So far, only Ireland has indicated that it is constitutionally bound to hold a referendum. The Lisbon Treaty would ideally streamline the decision making process of the EU and abolish the rotating Presidency of the Council, replacing it with a more permanent President of the Council. The Lisbon Treaty would also combine the role of the High Representative for Common Foreign and Security Policy, currently Javier Solana, and the EU Commissioner for External Relations, currently Benita Ferrero-Walder, into a single position, in an effort to combine the face and the purse strings of European foreign policy.

The European Commission

The role and responsibilities of the European Commission place it at the center of the EU's decision-making process. Acting as the EU's policy and executive engine, the Commission is composed of 25 Commissioners, one from each Member State and is supported by a substantial staff located primarily in Brussels, Belgium. In matters relating to economic integration ("First or 'Community' Pillar"), only the Commission has the right to propose legislation for approval by the EU Council and European Parliament. As "guardian of the Treaties," the Commission ensures that EU laws are applied and upheld throughout the EU, prosecuting Member States and other institutions for failing to follow treaty precepts or otherwise apply Community law. The Commission has full authority to enforce Community competition policy, and its policing of implementation of Community legislation preserves the integrity of the EU single market. The Commission likewise manages and develops the Common Agriculture Policy (CAP), implements the budget, and represents the European Community in its areas of competence, notably including international trade negotiations.

The Commission President is appointed by agreement of the EU heads of government and is subject to approval by the European Parliament. Commissioners serve for a renewable five-year term. New Commissioners are identified by Member State governments in consultation with the President-designate of the Commission and are normally put in place at the beginning of the term of the Commission President. The entire Commission must be confirmed as a collective whole by the European Parliament before its formal appointment by common accord of EU governments.

The European Council

The Council of Ministers of the European Union (the "EU Council") is the body in which representatives of the individual Member State governments, usually ministers, legislate for the EU, set its political objectives, coordinate national policies and resolve differences among their governments and with other EU bodies. Legally speaking, there is only one Council, but it meets in nine different formations, depending on the matters on its agenda.

Foreign ministers usually meet at least once a month in the General Affairs and External Relations Council (GAERC), which deals with major foreign policy issues and plays a coordinating role. Ministers for the Economy and Finance (ECOFIN) and ministers responsible for agriculture also hold monthly meetings. Ministers for Justice and Home Affairs (JHA) hold regular meetings to coordinate policies within their competence.

The Council holds formal sessions in its Brussels headquarters, except in April, June and October, when all sessions take place in Luxembourg. Most formations of the Council also meet informally (tasking no legally binding decisions) in the country holding the EU Presidency, usually once in the course of the Presidency's six-month term. The most prominent of these informal meetings is the so-called "Gymnich" meeting of foreign ministers, named for a town in Germany where the first such meeting took place.

The Council takes most decisions under the Community Pillar by qualified majority voting (QMV) but endeavors to reach the broadest possible consensus before approving legislation. Unanimity is required for a number of specific areas related to economic integration (e.g. taxation), constitutional matters such as amendments to the treaties, the launching of a new common policy, the accession of a new Member State, and matters falling within the EU's Common Foreign and Security Policy, European Security and Defense Policy, and aspects of law enforcement and judicial cooperation. The number of votes cast by each Member State when the EU Council votes by qualified majority voting was determined by the Nice Treaty and roughly correlates to the size of its population.

ECONOMY

The institutions of the European Union were originally created to oversee the operation of the several economic communities that later became the Single European Market. Even as the EU's political integration has continued, the area of greatest integration has always been in the economic sphere: goods, capital, and labor move freely between Member States (with some exceptions), businesses in all Member States are increasingly subject to common basic rules, and 16 of the 27 Member States use a common currency, the euro. The 16 euro-area countries share a common monetary policy administered by the European Central Bank in Frankfurt, Germany. The EU strives to eliminate internal barriers to the free flow of goods, services, labor, and capital, and to promote the overall convergence of living standards. Internationally, the EU aims to strengthen Europe's trade position and capitalize on the political and economic leverage that a large, unified market brings.

Growth

The EU is the world's largest economic area (the U.S. is second) with an estimated 2008 GDP (Purchasing Power Parity) of $14.96 trillion; however, growth is expected to drop significantly in 2009, with many members experiencing recession. Within the euro area, growth varies as much as 9.5 percentage points between the fastest and slowest-growing economies. In 2008, many of the EU's largest economies, including Germany, France and Italy, will grow by less than two percent. Outside the euro area, several members will experience sharp contractions. Hungary and Latvia have sought IMF assistance in the wake of financial crises.

In spring 2000, the EU committed to a ten-year strategic goal of transforming the EU into a more competitive, knowledge-based economy capable of sustaining higher levels of growth. Focusing on labor market reform, macroeconomic and fiscal policy, and promotion of e-commerce and entrepreneurship, the EU's "Lisbon Agenda" was an attempt to stimulate growth while remaining committed to the EU social model. Some suggest that it has so far failed to achieve its goals in large part because national governments (which retain authority over employment policy, immigration, large public sector workforces, entitlement programs and pensions) have not completed the necessary reforms. With euro area unemployment at 7.4 percent in 2007, generous social programs continue to strain national economies.

Fiscal and Monetary Policy

Introduced in 1999, the euro is currently the official currency of sixteen of the 27 EU Member States. United Kingdom, Denmark and Sweden chose to retain their national currencies, and most newer EU members have yet to adopt the euro. Prior to the euro's launch in 1999, national currency exchange rates of countries intending to join the euro were fixed within an Exchange Rate Mechanism. Following the January 2002 introduction of euro notes and coins into general circulation, national currencies were removed from circulation. Each of the euro area countries agreed to abide by a shared fiscal policy rule book known as the Stability and Growth Pact (SGP). This agreement generally obliges national governments to limit government budget deficits to 3 percent of GDP and established a target debt-to-GDP ratio of below sixty percent. Although enforcement actions have been forgiving - France and Germany, for example, avoided sanctions despite missing SGP targets - countries violating the SGP are technically subject to sanctions by the European Commission. National governments have been granted budget leeway to achieve structural reforms and to combat prolonged stagnation, negative growth or other factors, such as the cost of German reunification or state pensions. The revised standards still require deficits to remain close to the targets; they may only temporarily exceed the three percent limit. Member States that joined the EU after May 2004 may adopt the euro after complying with the SGP targets and meeting other applicable criteria. Four of the twelve new member states have already done so (Slovenia - January 1, 2007; Cyprus and Malta - January 1, 2008; and Slovakia - January 1, 2009).

The euro area's monetary policy is set by the European Central Bank (ECB), which must accommodate a wide range of domestic policies and economic conditions within euro area Member States. The Treaties require that the ECB's primary objective be to maintain price stability (i.e., to keep inflation low). Euro-area national governments have sometimes criticized the ECB for guarding against inflation at the expense of growth. The ECB changed its monetary stance following the severe deterioration of the financial situation in September-October 2008, cutting its refinancing rate three times in an attempt to stimulate bank lending.

Trade
The EU is the world's largest exporter of goods and services, and the U.S. is the EU's main trading partner by a wide margin. In 2007, the U.S. consisted of 12.7% of all goods imports to the EU. U.S. goods and services exports to the EU reached $395 billion in 2007, while U.S. goods and services imports from the EU totaled $511 billion. Asian economies such as Japan and China, however, account for an increasingly important share of EU trade. The EU's two-way merchandise trade with China grew to $388 billion in 2007, while merchandise trade with Japan was $156 billion.

Foreign Direct Investment
The U.S. is the largest investor in the EU, and EU countries are collectively the largest investors in the U.S. The EU is both a major destination for foreign direct investment (FDI) and a major source of FDI. U.S. foreign direct investment in the EU totaled $1.4 trillion in 2007, representing 49.3% of total U.S. FDI; EU FDI in the U.S. totaled $1.3 trillion, representing 62% of total foreign investment in the U.S. Growth of intra-EU FDI has increased rapidly in recent years and has increased much faster than FDI in non-EU countries.

www.ingramcontent.com/pod-product-compliance
Lightning Source LLC
Chambersburg PA
CBHW051318170526
45166CB00002B/592